THE AUTHOR: Makoto Ueda is Professor of Japanese and Comparative Literature at Stanford University. Born in Japan in 1931, he graduated from Kobe University in 1954. He completed his graduate work in the United States, receiving a master's degree from the University of Nebraska in 1956 and a doctorate from the University of Washington in 1961. He has also taught at the University of Washington, Indiana University, and the University of Toronto. His articles and translations have appeared in many journals, such as *The Chicago Review*, *The Sewanee Review*, and *Beloit Poetry Journal*. Besides the present volume, he has published seven books, including *Literary and Art Theories in Japan* (1967), *Modern Japanese Haiku: An Anthology* (1976), and *Modern Japanese Writers and the Nature of Literature* (1976).

MATSUO BASHŌ

By MAKOTO UEDA

KODANSHA INTERNATIONAL
Tokyo • New York • London

Previously published by Twayne Publishers, Inc. in 1970.

Distributed in the United States by Kodansha America, Inc., 114 Fifth Avenue, New York, N.Y. 10011, and in the United Kingdom and continental Europe by Kodansha Europe Ltd., 95 Aldwych, London WC2B 4JF. Published by Kodansha International Ltd., 17-14 Otowa 1-chome, Bunkyo-ku, Tokyo 112, and Kodansha America, Inc. Printed in Japan.

LCC 82-48165
ISBN 0-87011-553-7
ISBN 4-7700-1051-6 (in Japan)

First paperback edition, 1982
94 95 96 97 98 12 11 10 9

Preface

The Japanese haiku, consisting of only seventeen syllables, is one of the shortest verse forms in world literature. It has become widely known in the West, especially since its conciseness and super-pository structure caught the interest of the Imagists early in this century. The influence of the haiku is noticeable in varying degrees in the poems of Ezra Pound, Amy Lowell, Wallace Stevens, William Carlos Williams, and other contemporary poets. Today, one need not be an eccentric to write a haiku in English. A large number of people, ranging from grade-school children to established poets, entertain themselves by writing verse in this form, and some of their products are very interesting indeed. There are several magazines in North America that regularly publish haiku in English.

The haiku which has the present 5-7-5 syllable pattern began in Japan in the sixteenth century and has been thriving ever since. Adorning its long history are a number of great poets who, with their various individual talents, have explored its poetic possibilities from many angles and have produced numerous masterpieces in the course of doing so. Yet if one poet is to be singled out as the greatest contributor to the development of haiku literature, there will be little question about the choice: it has to be Matsuo Bashō. Before Bashō's time the haiku had not realized its full potential and was regarded as little more than an entertaining pastime. With Bashō it came to maturity and attained the status of a major literary genre. And from that time on Bashō was the authoritative model, a poet of the highest order whose presence could never be ignored by anyone writing in that genre. Those who wanted to write in a radically different style had to deny Bashō's poetry first and justify their denial in one way or another.

This book is intended to give a comprehensive view of Bashō's works in the haiku as well as in other related forms in which he wrote. After a brief look at his life, it traces his gradual growth as a haiku poet, showing the ways his poetic genius was manifested at different stages of his career. It proceeds to an analysis of two samples from his *renku,* or linked verse, an interesting verse form out of which the haiku evolved. This is followed by a discussion of Bashō's prose, for he was a fine prose writer who produced a number of short poetic essays and a few travel journals. Also treated is his literary criticism which marked a high point in the history of Japanese esthetics. The book ends with a glance at Bashō's influence on later literature.

Although some of his works are available in English (and he is one of the more fortunate Japanese poets in this regard), they represent only a small part of the vast Bashō canon. Extant translations are scarce, especially in the areas of the renku and literary criticism. This book tries to cite Bashō's works in translation as much as possible, for there is little sense in analyzing a work that is not available in English. It is for this reason that the third chapter cites two linked poems (hitherto untranslated) in their entirety even though they are rather lengthy. Fortunately, the haiku is much shorter and far more quotable: about one hundred and sixty haiku are included in the following pages.

A clarification of several literary terms is in order. In this book, the term "haiku" is used in accordance with today's Japanese usage: it designates an independent, autonomous verse written in the 5-7-5 syllable pattern. The word "hokku," on the other hand, refers to the opening verse of a linked poem; though it has the same form as the haiku, it anticipates other verses to follow and to complement its meaning. In Bashō's day "hokku" was a more inclusive term and covered the realm of today's haiku as well; he and his contemporaries seldom used the word haiku, even though, as seen in Bashō's journals, the practice of treating a hokku as an independent poem was common. To avoid unnecessary confusion, this book employs the term haiku for any self-contained 5-7-5 syllable poem. Finally, the word haikai is used as a general term encompassing the whole range of haiku literature; it includes the haiku, the renku, and prose written in the spirit of the haiku. In other words, the term is so broad as to cover the entire scope of Bashō's writings, and that the scope of this book also.

I am indebted to many persons in the writing of this book. Indeed, there is virtually no page in this book that does not owe something to the awesome collection of Japanese Bashō studies. From an almost endless list of names I should at least mention, with deep gratitude, some of the more recent Japanese scholars whose works I found especially helpful: Abe Kimio, Asano Shin, Asō Isoji, Iino Tetsuji, Imoto Nōichi, Iwata Kurō, Katō Shūson, Kon Eizō, Konishi Jin'ichi, Kuriyama Riichi, Miyamoto Saburō, Nakamura Shunjō, Namimoto Sawaichi, Ogata Tsutomu, Okazaki Yoshie, Ōtani Tokuzō, Ōuchi Hatsuo, Yamaguchi Seishi, and Yamamoto Kenichi (throughout this book Japanese names are given in the Japanese order, the surname coming before the personal name). I am equally grateful to Western scholars whose works I consulted in the course of my research: I found most of their translations very conscientious —some of them superb, indeed—and it was only for the sake of stylistic uniformity that I translated all quotations from Bashō myself. I have, however, borrowed from Nobuyuki Yuasa his English rendering of the titles of Bashō's travel journals. Mrs. Jan Goodman kindly read my manuscript and offered many helpful suggestions. My thanks are also due to those on the library staff at the University of Toronto, Stanford University and the University of California, Berkeley, for helping me locate materials during my research. Last but not least, I thank Professor Roy Teele for suggesting that I write this book.

M.U.

Chronology

1644 Matsuo Bashō born at or near Ueno in Iga Province.
1656 His father's death. Probably by this time Bashō had entered the service of Tōdō Yoshitada, a young relative of the feudal lord ruling the area.
1662 Wrote his earliest verse extant today.
1666 Yoshitada's death. Basho resigned and entered a long period of unsettled life. He may have gone to live in Kyoto for a time.
1672 Dedicated *The Seashell Game* to a shrine in Ueno. Later moved to Edo in search of a new career.
1676 Wrote a pair of hundred-verse renku with another poet in Edo. Paid a brief visit to Ueno in the summer.
1678 Wrote critical commentaries for *Haiku Contests in Eighteen Rounds.*
1680 *Best Poems of Tōsei's Twenty Disciples* published. Judged "The Rustic Haiku Contest" and "The Evergreen Haiku Contest." Settled in the initial Bashō Hut.
1682 The Bashō Hut destroyed by fire. He took refuge in Kai Province for a few months.
1683 *Shriveled Chestnuts* compiled. His mother died in Ueno. New Bashō Hut built.
1684–1685 Went on a journey that resulted in *The Records of a Weather-Exposed Skeleton.* In Nagoya he led a team of poets to produce *The Winter Sun.*
1686 Wrote what is now known as *Critical Notes on the New Year's Renku.*
1687 Traveled to Kashima and wrote *A Visit to Kashima Shrine.* Judged one of the haiku contests published in *The Extending Plain.*
1687 Undertook a journey which produced *The Records of*

a Travel-Worn Satchel and *A Visit to Sarashina Village.*

1688 Returned to Edo in the autumn of 1688.

1689 Journeyed in northern provinces of Honshu. The journey provided material for *The Narrow Road to the Deep North,* which he completed some time later.

1690 Visited friends and disciples in the Kyoto area. Stayed at the Unreal Hut near Lake Biwa for several months during the summer.

1691 Stayed at the House of Fallen Persimmons for a couple of weeks in the summer and wrote *The Saga Diary. The Monkey's Cloak* published. Returned to Edo toward the end of the year.

1692 The third Bashō Hut built. Wrote a haibun about the transplanting of banana trees.

1693 Wrote what is known as *Autumn Night Critical Commentaries.* Closed his gate and declined to see visitors for a time.

1694 *A Sack of Charcoal* published. Set out for another long journey in the summer. Fell ill and died in Osaka in early autumn.

Contents

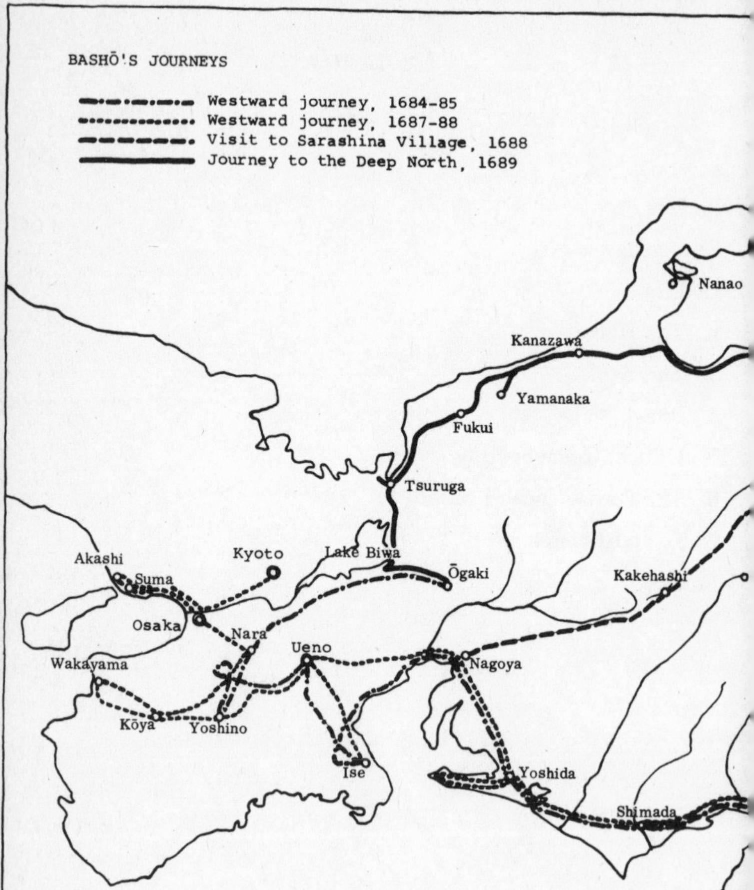
BASHŌ'S JOURNEYS
Westward journey, 1684-85
Westward journey, 1687-88
Visit to Sarashina Village, 1688
Journey to the Deep North, 1689
Nanao
Kanazawa
Yamanaka
Fukui
Tsuruga
Akashi
Kyoto
Lake Biwa
Ōgaki
Suma
Kakehashi
Osaka
Nara
Ueno
Nagoya
Wakayama
Kōya
Yoshino
Ise
Yoshida
Shimada

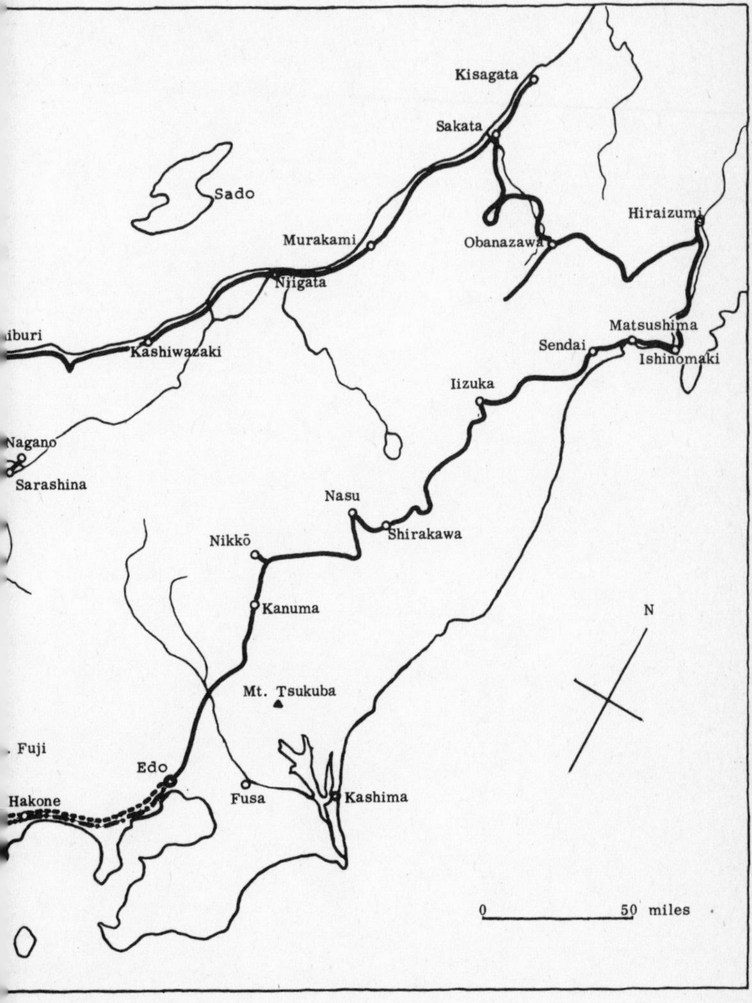
Kisagata
Sakata
Sado
Murakami
Obanazawa
Hiraizumi
Niigata
iburi
Kashiwazaki
Matsushima
Sendai
Ishinomaki
Iizuka
Nagano
Sarashina
Nasu
Shirakawa
Nikkō
Kanuma
N
Mt. Tsukuba
Fuji
Edo
Hakone
Fusa
Kashima
0
50 miles

CHAPTER 1

Life

ONE DAY in the spring of 1681 a banana tree was seen being planted alongside a modest hut in a rustic area of Edo, a city now known as Tokyo. It was a gift from a local resident to his teacher of poetry, who had moved into the hut several months earlier. The teacher, a man about thirty-six years of age, was delighted with the gift. He loved the banana plant because it was somewhat like him in the way it stood there. Its large leaves were soft and sensitive and were easily torn when gusty winds blew from the sea. Its flowers were small and unobtrusive; they looked lonesome, as if they knew they could bear no fruit in the cool climate of Japan. Its stalks were long and fresh-looking, yet they were of no practical use.

The teacher lived all alone in the hut. On nights when he had no visitor, he would sit quietly and listen to the wind blowing through the banana leaves. The lonely atmosphere would deepen on rainy nights. Rainwater leaking through the roof dripped intermittently into a basin. To the ears of the poet sitting in the dimly lighted room, the sound made a strange harmony with the rustling of the banana leaves outside.

Bashō nowaki shite	A banana plant in the autumn gale—
Tarai ni ame o	I listen to the dripping of rain
Kiku yo kana	Into a basin at night.

The haiku seems to suggest the poet's awareness of his spiritual affinity with the banana plant.

Some people who visited this teacher of poetry may have noticed the affinity. Others may have seen the banana plant as nothing more than a convenient landmark. At any rate, they came to call the residence the Bashō ("banana plant") Hut, and the name was soon applied to its resident, too: the teacher came to be known as the Master of the Bashō Hut, or Master Bashō. It goes without saying that he was happy to accept the nickname. He used it for the rest of his life.

I *First Metamorphosis: From Wanderer to Poet*

Little material is available to recreate Bashō's life prior to his settlement in the Bashō Hut. It is believed that he was born in 1644 at or near Ueno in Iga Province, about thirty miles southeast of Kyoto and two hundred miles west of Edo. He was called Kinsaku and several other names as a child; he had an elder brother and four sisters. His father, Matsuo Yozaemon, was probably a low-ranking samurai who farmed in peacetime. Little is known about his mother except that her parents were not natives of Ueno. The social status of the family, while respectable, was not of the kind that promised a bright future for young Bashō if he were to follow an ordinary course of life.

Yet Bashō's career began in an ordinary enough way. It is presumed that as a youngster he entered the service of a youthful master, Tōdō Yoshitada, a relative of the feudal lord ruling the province. Young Bashō first served as a page or in some such capacity.[1] His master, two years his senior, was apparently fond of Bashō, and the two seem to have become fairly good companions as they grew older. Their strongest bond was the haikai, one of the favorite pastimes of sophisticated men of the day. Apparently Yoshitada had a liking for verse writing and even acquired a haikai name, Sengin. Whether or not the initial stimulation came from his master, Bashō also developed a taste for writing haikai, using the pseudonym Sōbō. The earliest poem by Bashō preserved today was written in 1662. In 1664, two haiku by Bashō and one by Yoshitada appeared in a verse anthology published in Kyoto. The following year Bashō, Yoshitada, and three others joined together and composed a renku of one hundred verses. Bashō contributed eighteen verses, his first remaining verses of this type.

Bashō's life seems to have been peaceful so far, and he might for the rest of his life have been a satisfied, low-ranking samurai who spent his spare time verse writing. He had already come of age and had assumed a samurai's name, Matsuo Munefusa. But in the summer of 1666 a series of incidents completely changed the course of his life. Yoshitada suddenly died a premature death. His younger brother succeeded him as the head of the clan and also as the husband of his widow. It is believed that Bashō left his native home and embarked on a wandering life shortly afterward.

Various surmises have been made as to the reasons for Bashō's decision to leave home, a decision that meant forsaking his samurai status. One reason which can be easily imagined is Bashō's deep grief at the death of his master, to whom he had been especially close. One early biography even has it that he thought of killing himself to accompany the master in the world beyond, but this was forbidden by the current law against self-immolation. Another and more convincing reason is that Bashō became extremely pessimistic about his future under the new master, whom he had never served before. As Yoshitada had Bashō, the new master must have had around him favored companions with whom he had been brought up. They may have tried to prevent Bashō from joining their circle, or even if they did not Bashō could have sensed some vague animosity in their attitudes toward him. Whatever the truth may have been, there seems to be no doubt that Bashō's future as a samurai became exceedingly clouded upon the sudden death of his master.

Other surmises about Bashō's decision to leave home have to do with his love affairs. Several early biographies claim that he had an affair with his elder brother's wife, with one of Yoshitada's waiting ladies, or with Yoshitada's wife herself. These are most likely the fabrications of biographers who felt the need for some sensational incident in the famous poet's youth. But there is one theory that may contain some truth. It maintains that Bashō had a secret mistress, who later became a nun called Jutei. She may even have had a child, or several children, by Bashō. At any rate, these accounts seem to point toward one fact: Bashō, still in his early twenties, experienced his share of the joys and griefs that most young men go through at one time or another.

Bashō's life for the next few years is very obscure. It has traditionally been held that he went to Kyoto, then the capital of Japan, where he studied philosophy, poetry, and calligraphy under well-known experts. It is not likely, however, that he was in Kyoto all during this time; he must often have returned to his home town for lengthy visits. It might even be that he still lived in Ueno or in that vicinity and made occasional trips to Kyoto. In all likelihood he was not yet determined to become a poet at this time. Later in his own writing he was to recall "At one time I coveted an official post with a tenure of land." He was still young and ambitious, confident of his potential. He must have wished, above all, to get a good education that would secure him some kind of respectable position later on. Perhaps he wanted to see the wide world outside his native town and to mix with a wide variety of people. With the curiosity of youth he may have tried to do all sorts of things fashionable among the young libertines of the day. Afterward he even wrote, "There was a time when I was fascinated with the ways of homosexual love."

One indisputable fact is that Bashō had not lost his interest in verse writing. A haikai anthology published in 1667 contained as many as thirty-one of his verses, and his work was included in three other anthologies compiled between 1669 and 1671. His name was gradually becoming known to a limited number of poets in the capital. That must have earned him considerable respect from the poets in his home town, too. Thus when Bashō made his first attempt to compile a book of haikai, about thirty poets were willing to contribute verses to it. The book, called *The Seashell Game* (*Kai Ōi*), was dedicated to a shrine in Ueno early in 1672.

The Seashell Game represents a haiku contest in thirty rounds. Pairs of haiku, each one composed by a different poet, are matched and judged by Bashō. Although he himself contributed two haiku to the contest, the main value of the book lies in his critical comments and the way he refereed the matches. On the whole, the book reveals him to be a man of brilliant wit and colorful imagination, who had a good knowledge of popular songs, fashionable expressions, and the new ways of the world in general. It appears he compiled the book in a lighthearted mood, but his poetic talent was evident.

Then, probably in the spring of 1672, Bashō set out on a journey to Edo, apparently with no intention of returning in the immediate future. On parting he sent a haiku to one of his friends in Ueno:

Kumo to hedatsu	Clouds will separate
Tomo ka ya kari no	The two friends, after the migrating
Ikiwakare	Wild goose's departure.

His motive for going to Edo cannot be ascertained. Now that he had some education, he perhaps wanted to find a promising post in Edo, then a fast-expanding city which offered a number of career opportunities. Or perhaps, encouraged by the good reception that *The Seashell Game* enjoyed locally, he had already made up his mind to become a professional poet and wanted his name known in Edo, too. Most likely Bashō had multiple motives, being yet a young man with plenty of ambition. Whether he wanted to be a government official or a haikai master, Edo seemed to be an easier place than Kyoto to realize his dreams. He was anxious to try out his potential in a different, freer environment.

Bashō's life for the next eight years is somewhat obscure again. It is said that in his early days in Edo he stayed at the home of one or another of his patrons. That is perhaps true, but it is doubtful that he could remain a dependent for long. Various theories, none of them with convincing evidence, argue that he became a physician's assistant, a town clerk, or a poet's scribe. The theory generally considered to be closest to the truth is that for some time he was employed by the local waterworks department. Whatever the truth, his early years in Edo were not easy. He was probably recalling those days when he later wrote: "At one time I was weary of verse writing and wanted to give it up, and at another time I was determined to be a poet until I could establish a proud name over others. The alternatives battled in my mind and made my life restless."

Though he may have been in a dilemma Bashō continued to write verses in the new city. In the summer of 1675 he was one of several writers who joined a distinguished poet of the time in composing a renku of one hundred verses; Bashō, now using the pseudonym Tōsei, contributed eight. The following spring he and another poet wrote two renku, each consisting of one hundred verses. After a brief visit to his native town later in the year, he began devoting more and more time to verse writing. He must have made up his mind to become a professional poet around this time, if he had not done so earlier. His work began appearing in various haikai anthologies more and more frequently, indicating his increasing renown. When the New Year came he apparently distributed a small book of verses among his acquaintances, a practice permitted only to a recognized haikai master. In the winter of that year he judged two haiku contests, and when they were published as *Haiku Contests in Eighteen Rounds (Jūhachiban Hokku Awase)*, he wrote a commentary on each match. In the summer of 1680 *The Best Poems of Tōsei's Twenty Disciples (Tōsei Montei Dokugin Nijikkasen)* appeared, which suggests that Bashō already had a sizable group of talented students. Later in the same year two of his leading disciples matched their own verses in two contests, "The Rustic Haiku Contest" ("Inaka no Kuawase") and "The Evergreen Haiku Contest" ("Tokiwaya no Kuawase"), and Bashō served as the judge. That winter his students built a small house in a quiet, rustic part of Edo and presented it to their teacher. Several months later a banana tree was planted in the yard, giving the hut its famous name. Bashō, firmly established as a poet, now had his own home for the first time in his life.

II *Second Metamorphosis: From Poet to Wanderer*

Bashō was thankful to have a permanent home, but he was not to be cozily settled there. With all his increasing poetic fame and material comfort, he seemed to become more dissatisfied with himself. In his early days of struggle he had had a concrete aim in life, a purpose to strive for. That aim, now virtually attained, did not seem to be worthy of all his effort. He had many friends, disciples, and patrons, and yet he was lonelier than ever. One of the first verses he wrote after moving into the Bashō Hut was:

Shiba no to ni	Against the brushwood gate
Cha o konoha kaku	Dead tea leaves swirl
Arashi kana	In the stormy wind.

Many other poems written at this time, including the haiku about the banana tree, also have pensive overtones. In a headnote to one of them he even wrote: "I feel lonely as I gaze at the moon, I feel lonely as I think about myself, and I feel lonely as I ponder upon this wretched life of mine. I want to cry out that I am lonely, but no one asks me how I feel."

It was probably out of such spiritual ambivalence that Bashō began practicing Zen meditation under Priest Butchō (1642–1715), who happened to be staying near his home. He must have been zealous and resolute in this attempt, for he was later to recall: ". . . and at another time I was anxious to confine myself within the walls of a monastery." Loneliness, melancholy, disillusion, ennui—whatever his problem may have been, his suffering was real.

A couple of events that occurred in the following two years further increased his suffering. In the winter of 1682 the Bashō Hut was destroyed in a fire that swept through the whole neighborhood. He was homeless again, and probably the idea that man is eternally homeless began haunting his mind more and more frequently. A few months later he received news from his family home that his mother had died. Since his father had died already in 1656, he was now not only without a home but without a parent to return to.

As far as poetic fame was concerned, Bashō and his disciples were thriving. In the summer of 1683 they published *Shriveled Chestnuts (Minashiguri)*, an anthology of haikai verses which, in its stern rejection of crudity and vulgarity in theme and in its highly articulate, Chinese-flavored diction, set them distinctly apart from other poets. In that winter, when the homeless Bashō returned from a stay in Kai Province, his friends and disciples again gathered together and presented him with a new Bashō Hut. He was pleased, but it was not enough to do away with his melancholy. His poem on entering the new hut was:

Arare kiku ya	The sound of hail—
Kono mi wa moto no	I am the same as before
Furugashiwa	Like that aging oak.

Neither poetic success nor the security of a home seemed to offer him much consolation. He was already a wanderer in spirit, and he had to follow that impulse in actual life.

Thus in the fall of 1684 Bashō set out on his first significant journey. He had made journeys before, but not for the sake of spiritual and poetic discipline. Through the journey he wanted, among other things, to face death and thereby to help temper his mind and his poetry. He called it "the journey of a weather-beaten skeleton," meaning that he was prepared to perish alone and leave his corpse to the mercies of the wilderness if that was his destiny. If this seems to us a bit extreme, we should remember that Bashō was of a delicate constitution and suffered from several chronic diseases, and that travel in seventeenth-century Japan was immensely more hazardous than it is today.

It was a long journey, taking him to a dozen provinces that lay between Edo and Kyoto. From Edo he went westward along a main road that more or less followed the Pacific coastline. He passed by the foot of Mount Fuji, crossed several large rivers, and visited the Grand Shinto Shrines in Ise. He then arrived at his native town, Ueno, and was reunited with his relatives and friends. His elder brother opened a memento bag and showed him a small tuft of gray hair from the head of his late mother.

Te ni toraba	Should I hold it in my hand
Kien namida zo atsuki	It would melt in my burning tears—
Aki no shimo	Autumnal frost.

This is one of the rare cases in which a poem bares his emotion, no doubt because the grief he felt was uncontrollably intense.

After only a few days' sojourn in Ueno, Bashō traveled farther on, now visiting a temple among the mountains, now composing verses with local poets. It was at this time that *The Winter Sun (Fuyu no Hi)*, a collection of five renku which with their less pedantic vocabulary and more lyrical tone marked the beginning of Bashō's mature poetic style, was produced. He then celebrated the New Year at his native town for the first time in years. He spent some more time visiting Nara and Kyoto, and when he finally returned to Edo it was already the summer of 1685.

The journey was a rewarding one. Bashō met numerous friends, old and new, on the way. He produced a number of haiku and renku on his experiences during the journey, including those collected in *The Winter Sun*. He wrote his first travel journal, *The Records of a Weather-Exposed Skeleton (Nozarashi Kikō)*, too. Through all these experiences, Bashō was gradually changing. In the latter part of the journal there appears, for instance, the following haiku which he wrote at the year's end:

Toshi kurenu	Another year is gone—
Kasa kite waraji	A travel hat on my head,
Hakinagara	Straw sandals on my feet.

The poem seems to show Bashō at ease in travel. The uneasiness that made him assume a strained attitude toward the journey disappeared as his trip progressed. He could now look at his wandering self more objectively, without heroism or sentimentalism.

He spent the next two years enjoying a quiet life at the Bashō Hut. It was a modest but leisurely existence, and he could afford to call himself "an idle old man." He contemplated the beauty of nature as it changed with the seasons and wrote verses whenever he was inspired to do so. Friends and disciples who visited him shared his taste, and they often gathered to enjoy the beauty of the moon, the snow, or the blossoms. The following composition, a short prose piece written in the winter of 1686, seems typical of his life at this time:

A man named Sora[2] has his temporary residence near my hut, so I often drop in at his place, and he at mine. When I cook something to eat he helps to feed the fire, and when I make tea at night he comes over for company. A quiet, leisurely person, he has become a most congenial friend of mine. One evening after a snowfall, he dropped in for a visit, whereupon I composed a haiku:

Kimi hi o take	Will you start a fire?
Yoki mono misen	I'll show you something nice—
Yukimaroge	A huge snowball.

The fire in the poem is to boil water for tea. Sora would prepare tea in the kitchen, while Bashō, returning to the pleasures of a little boy, would make a big snowball in the yard. When the tea was ready, they would sit down and sip it together, humorously enjoying the view of the snowball outside. The poem, an unusually cheerful one for Bashō, seems to suggest his relaxed, carefree frame of mind of those years.

The same sort of casual poetic mood led Bashō to undertake a short trip to Kashima, a town about fifty miles east of Edo and well known for its Shinto shrine, to see the harvest moon. Sora and a certain Zen monk accompanied him in the trip in the autumn of 1687. Unfortunately it rained on the night of the full moon, and they had only a few glimpses of the moon toward dawn. Bashō, however, took advantage of the chance to visit his former Zen master, Priest Butchō, who had retired to Kashima. The trip resulted in another of Bashō's travel journals, *A Visit to the Kashima Shrine (Kashima Kikō).*

Then, just two months later, Bashō set out on another long westward journey. He was far more at ease as he took leave than he had been at the outset of his first such journey three years earlier. He was a famous poet now, with a large circle of friends and disciples. They gave him many farewell presents, invited him to picnics and dinners, and arranged several verse-writing parties in his honor. Those who could not attend sent their poems. These verses, totaling nearly three hundred and fifty, were later collected and published under the title *Farewell Verses* (*Kusenbetsu*). There were so many festivities that to Bashō "the occasion looked like some dignitary's departure—very imposing indeed."

He followed roughly the same route as on his journey of 1684, again visiting friends and writing verses here and there on the way. He reached Ueno at the year's end and was heartily welcomed as a leading poet in Edo. Even the young head of his former master's family, whose service he had left in his youth, invited him for a visit. In the garden a cherry tree which Yoshitada had loved was in full bloom.

Samazama no	Myriads of things past
Koto omoidasu	Are brought to my mind—
Sakura kana	These cherry blossoms!

In the middle of the spring Bashō left Ueno, accompanied by one of his students, going first to Mount Yoshino to see the famous cherry blossoms. He traveled on to Wakanoura to enjoy the spring scenes of the Pacific coast, and then came to Nara at the time of fresh green leaves. On he went to Osaka, and then to Suma and Akashi on the coast of Seto Inland Sea, two famous places which often appeared in old Japanese classics.

From Akashi Bashō turned back to the east, and by way of Kyoto arrived at Nagoya in midsummer. After resting there for awhile, he headed for the mountains of central Honshu, an area now popularly known as the Japanese Alps. An old friend of his and a servant, loaned to him by someone who worried about the steep roads ahead, accompanied Bashō. His immediate purpose was to see the harvest moon in the rustic Sarashina district. As expected, the trip was a rugged one, but he did see the full moon at that place celebrated in Japanese literature. He then traveled eastward among the mountains and returned to Edo in late autumn after nearly a year of traveling.

This was probably the happiest of all Bashō's journeys. He had been familiar with the route much of the way, and where he had not, a friend and a servant had been there to help him. His fame as a poet was fairly widespread, and people he met on the way always treated him with courtesy. It was a productive journey, too. In addition to a number of haiku and renku, he wrote two journals: *The Records of a Travel-Worn Satchel (Oi no Kobumi)*, which covers his travel from Edo to Akashi, and *A Visit to Sarashina Village (Sarashina Kikō)*, which focuses on his moon-viewing trip to Sarashina. The former has an especially significant place in the Bashō canon, including among other things a passage that declares the haikai to be among the major forms of Japanese art. He was now clearly aware of the significance of haikai writing; he was confident that the haikai, as a serious form of art, could point toward an invaluable way of life.

It was no wonder, then, that Bashō began preparing for the next journey almost immediately. As he described it, it was as if the God of Travel were beckoning him. Obsessed with the charms of a traveler's life, he now wanted to go beyond his previous journeys; he wanted to be a truer wanderer than ever before. In a letter written around this time, he says he admired the life of a monk who wanders about with only a begging bowl in his hand. Bashō now wanted to travel, not as a renowned poet, but as a self-disciplining monk. Thus in the pilgrimage to come he decided to visit the northern part of Honshu, a mostly rustic and in places even wild region where he had never been and had hardly an acquaintance. He was to cover about fifteen hundred miles on the way. Of course, it was going to be the longest journey of his life.

Accompanied by Sora, Bashō left Edo in the late spring of 1689. Probably because of his more stern and ascetic attitude toward the journey, farewell festivities were fewer and quieter this time.

He proceeded northward along the main road, stopping at places of interest such as the Tōshō Shrine at Nikkō, the hot spa at Nasu, and an historic castle site at Iizuka. He then came close to the Pacific coast near Sendai and admired the scenic beauty of Matsushima. From Hiraizumi, a town well known as the site of a medieval battle, Bashō turned west and reached the coast of the Sea of Japan at Sakata. After a short trip to Kisagata in the north, he turned southwest and followed the main road along the cosat. It was from this coast that he saw the island of Sado in the distance and wrote one of his most celebrated poems:

Araumi ya	The rough sea—
Sado ni yokotau	Extending toward Sado Isle,
Amanogawa	The Milky Way.

Because of the rains, the heat, and the rugged road, this part of the journey was very hard for Bashō and Sora, and they were both exhausted when they finally arrived at Kanazawa. They rested at the famous hot spring at Yamanaka for a few days, but Sora, apparently because of prolonged ill-health, decided to give up the journey and left his master there. Bashō continued alone until he reached Fukui. There he met an old acquaintance, who accompanied him as far as Tsuruga, where another old friend had come to meet Bashō, and the two traveled south until they arrived at Ōgaki, a town Bashō knew well. A number of Bashō's friends and disciples were there, and the long journey through unfamiliar areas was finally over. One hundred and fifty-six days had passed since he left Edo.

The travel marked a climax in Bashō's literary career. He wrote some of his finest haiku during the journey. The resulting journal, *The Narrow Road to the Deep North (Oku no Hosomichi),* is one of the highest attainments in the history of poetic diaries in Japan. His literary achievement was no doubt a result of his deepening maturity as a man. He had come to perceive a mode of life by which to resolve some deep dilemmas and to gain peace of mind. It was based on the idea of *sabi,* the concept that one attains perfect spiritual serenity by immersing oneself in the egoless, impersonal life of nature. The complete absorption of one's petty ego into the vast, powerful, magnificent universe—this was the underlying theme of many poems by Bashō at this time, including the haiku on the Milky Way we have just seen. This momentary identification of man with inanimate nature was, in his view, essential to poetic creation. Though he never wrote a treatise on the subject, there is no doubt that Bashō conceived some unique ideas about poetry in his later years. Apparently it was during this journey that he began thinking about poetry in more serious, philosophical terms. The two earliest books known to record Bashō's thoughts on poetry, *Records of the Seven Days (Kikigaki Nanukagusa)* and *Conversations at Yamanaka* (*Yamanaka Mondō*), resulted from it.

Bashō spent the next two years visiting his old friends and disciples in Ueno, Kyoto, and towns on the southern coast of Lake Biwa. With one or another of them he often paid a brief visit to other places such as Ise and Nara. Of numerous houses he stayed at during this period Bashō seems to have especially enjoyed two: the Unreal Hut and the House of Fallen Persimmons, as they were called. The Unreal Hut, located in the woods off the southernmost tip of Lake Biwa, was a quiet, hidden place where Bashō rested from early summer to mid-autumn in 1690. He thoroughly enjoyed the idle, secluded life there, and described it in a short but superb piece of prose. Here is one of the passages:

> In the daytime an old watchman from the local shrine or some villager from the foot of the hill comes along and chats with me about things I rarely hear of, such as a wild boar's looting the rice paddies or a hare's haunting the bean farms. When the sun sets under the edge of the hill and night falls, I quietly sit and wait for the moon. With the moonrise I begin roaming about, casting my shadow on the ground. When the night deepens I return to the hut and meditate on right and wrong, gazing at the dim margin of a shadow in the lamplight.

Bashō had another chance to live a similarly secluded life later at the House of Fallen Persimmons in Saga, a northwestern suburb of Kyoto. The house, owned by one of his disciples, Mukai Kyorai (1651–1704), was so called because persimmon trees grew around it. There were also a number of bamboo groves, which provided the setting for a well-known poem by Bashō:

Hototogisu	The cuckoo—

Ōtakeyabu o	Through the dense bamboo grove,
Moru tsukiyo	Moonlight seeping.

Bashō stayed at this house for seventeen days in the summer of 1691. The sojourn resulted in *The Saga Diary (Saga Nikki),* the last of his longer prose works.

All during this period at the two hideaways and elsewhere in the Kyoto-Lake Biwa area, Bashō was visited by many people who shared his interest in poetry. Especially close to him were two of his leading disciples, Kyorai and Nozawa Bonchō (16?–1714), partly because they were compiling a haikai anthology under Bashō's guidance. The anthology, entitled *The Monkey's Cloak (Sarumino)* and published in the early summer of 1691, represented a peak in the haikai of the Bashō style. Bashō's idea of sabi and other principles of verse writing that evolved during his journey to the far north were clearly there. Through actual examples the new anthology showed that the haikai could be a serious art form capable of embodying mature comments on man and his environment.

Bashō returned to Edo in the winter of 1691. His friends and disciples there, who had not seen him for more than two years, welcomed him warmly. For the third time they combined their efforts to build a hut for their master, who had given up the old one before his latest journey. In this third Bashō Hut, however, he could not enjoy the peaceful life he desired. For one thing, he now had a few people to look after. An invalid nephew had come to live with Bashō, who took care of him until his death in the spring of 1693. A woman by the name of Jutei, with whom Bashō apparently had had some special relationship in his youth, also seems to have come under his care at this time. She too was in poor health, and had several young children besides. Even apart from these involvements, Basho was becoming extremely busy, no doubt due to his great fame as a poet. Many people wanted to visit him, or invited him for visits. For instance, in a letter presumed to have been written on the eighth of the twelfth month, 1693, he told one prospective visitor that he would not be at home on the ninth, tenth, eleventh, twelfth, fourteenth, fifteenth, and sixteenth, suggesting that the visitor come either on the thirteenth or the eighteenth.[3] In another letter written about the same time, he bluntly said: "Disturbed by others, I have no peace of mind." That New Year he composed this haiku:

Toshidoshi ya	Year after year
Saru ni kisetaru	On the monkey's face,
Saru no men	A monkey's mask.

The poem has a touch of bitterness unusual for Bashō. He was dissatisfied with the progress that he (and possibly some of his students) was making.

As these responsibilities pressed on him, Bashō gradually became somewhat nihilistic. He had become a poet in order to transcend worldly involvements, but now he found himself deeply involved in worldly affairs precisely because of his poetic fame. The solution was either to renounce being a poet or to stop seeing people altogether. Bashō first tried the former, but to no avail. "I have tried to give up poetry and remain silent," he said, "but every time I did so a poetic sentiment would solicit my heart and something would flicker in my mind. Such is the magic spell of poetry." He had become too much of a poet. Thus he had to resort to the second alternative: to stop seeing people altogether. This he did in the autumn of 1693, declaring:

> Whenever people come, there is useless talk. Whenever I go and visit, I have the unpleasant feeling of interfering with other men's business. Now I can do nothing better than follow the examples of Sun Ching and Tu Wu-lang,[4] who confined themselves within locked doors. Friendlessness will become my friend, and poverty my wealth. A stubborn man at fifty years of age, I thus write to discipline myself.

Asagao ya	The morning-glory—
Hiru wa jō orosu	In the daytime, a bolt is fastened
Mon no kaki	On the frontyard gate.

Obviously, Bashō wished to admire the beauty of the morning-glory without having to keep a bolt on his gate. How to manage to do this must have been the subject of many hours of meditation within the locked house. He solved the problem, at least to his own satisfaction, and reopened the gate about a month after closing it.

Bashō's solution was based on the principle of "lightness," a dialectic transcendence of sabi. Sabi urges man to detach himself from worldly involvements; "lightness" makes it possible for him, after attaining that detachment, to return to the mundane world. Man lives amid the mire as a spiritual bystander. He does not escape the grievances of living; standing apart, he just smiles them away. Bashō began writing under this principle and advised his students to emulate him. The effort later came to fruition in several haikai anthologies, such as *A Sack of Charcoal (Sumidawara)*, *The Detached Room* (*Betsuzashiki*), and *The Monkey's Cloak, Continued* (*Zoku Sarumino*). Characteristic verses in these collections reject sentimentalism and take a calm, carefree attitude to the things of daily life. They often exude lighthearted humor.

Having thus restored his mental equilibrium, Bashō began thinking of another journey. He may have been anxious to carry his new poetic principle, "lightness," to poets outside of Edo, too. Thus in the summer of 1694 he traveled westward on the familiar road along the Pacific coast, taking with him one of Jutei's children, Jirōbei. He rested at Ueno for a while, and then visited his students in Kyoto and in towns near the southern coast of Lake Biwa. Jutei, who had been struggling against ill health at the Bashō Hut, died at this time and Jirōbei temporarily returned to Edo. Much saddened, Bashō went back to Ueno in early autumn for about a month's rest. He then left for Osaka with a few friends and relatives including his elder brother's son Mataemon as well as Jirōbei. But Bashō's health was rapidly failing, even though he continued to write some excellent verses. One of his haiku in Osaka was:

Kono aki wa	This autumn
Nan de toshiyoru	Why am I aging so?
Kumo ni tori	Flying towards the clouds, a bird.

The poem indicates Bashō's awareness of approaching death. Shortly afterward he took to his bed with a stomach ailment, from which he was not to recover. Numerous disciples hurried to Osaka and gathered at his bedside. He seems to have remained calm in his last days. He scribbled a deathbed note to his elder brother, which in part read: "I am sorry to have to leave you now. I hope you will live a happy life under Mataemon's care and reach a ripe old age. There is nothing more I have to say." The only thing that disturbed his mind was poetry. According to a disciple's record, Bashō fully knew that it was time for prayers, not for verse writing, and yet he thought of the latter day and night. Poetry was now an obsession—"a sinful attachment," as he himself called it. His last poem was:

Tabi ni yande	On a journey, ailing—
Yume wa kareno o	My dreams roam about
Kakemeguru	Over a withered moor.

CHAPTER 2

The Haiku

EXTANT HAIKU that are known to be Bashō's number about one thousand. The number must be said to be rather small, in view of the extreme brevity of the form.[1] Obviously, Bashō was not a prolific poet; for one thing, he took such meticulous care in selecting words and expressions. Yet his haiku, when viewed collectively, display a surprisingly wide range of themes and styles. This is because he constantly cultivated new poetic possibilities; like every major poet, he never stopped growing.

For convenience's sake, Bashō's growth as poet can be divided into five stages. The first is his early apprenticeship period, extending up to his departure for Edo in 1672. Bashō was in his twenties, and the haiku was for him little more than an entertaining pastime. The second stage covers his life in Edo up to his settlement in the initial Bashō Hut in 1680. Now in his thirties, he was busily learning from the new trends that were in vogue in that fast-expanding city. The third stage, spanning the years from 1681 to 1685, finds Bashō gradually separating himself from other poets and searching for his identity as poet. The fourth stage represents the peak of his literary activities, from 1686 to 1691. It was in this period that he established a unique style and thereby attracted a number of followers. The fifth stage, comprising the last three years of his life, illuminates the final phase of Basho's poetic evolution. Though a famed poet already, he was still not satisfied with himself and his work, and he persisted in efforts to improve his poetry to the very end.

In the following pages we shall try to trace these five stages, using representative examples of his haiku. In doing so we cannot overemphasize that these stages have been set up for the sake of convenience, and that the characteristics suggested for each are only generalizations. The scope and versatility of Bashō's haiku are far too great to fit into any neat pattern.

I *Haiku as Pastime: 1662–72*

Of all the haiku by Bashō that can be dated today, the earliest is the one he wrote in the winter of 1662 at the age of eighteen.[2] The date was the twenty-ninth of the twelfth month, popularly known as the Second Last Day, as it was two days before the New Year. That year it happened that the first day of spring, which usually came with the New Year, arrived early and fell on the Second Last Day. Therefore young Bashō's haiku:

Haru ya koshi	Was it spring that came,
Toshi ya yukiken	Or was it the year that went?
Kotsugomori	The Second Last Day.

The poem is rather trite and contrived, for it centers on a pretended confusion at a slightly unusual coincidence. The motif had often been dealt with by earlier poets, of whom the most notable was Ariwara Motokata (888-953) in this *tanka* or traditional thirty-one-syllable poem:

Toshi no uchi ni	Before the year is over
Haru wa kinikeri	Springtime has come.
Hitotose o	The remainder of the year,
Kozo to ya iwamu	Shall we call it last year
Kotoshi to ya iwamu	Or shall we call it this year?

To enliven this hackneyed theme, Bashō playfully borrowed a phrase from a famous love poem that appears in *The Tales of Ise (Ise Monogatari)*, one of the classics of Japanese court literature. The tanka, sent by a woman to a man after their first love-meeting, sang of her sweet lingering memory of the night:

Kimi ya koshi	Was it you who came
Ware ya yukikemu	Or was it I who went–
Omooezu	I do not remember.
Yume ka utsutsu ka	Was that dream or reality?
Nete ka samete ka	Was I asleep or awake?

Bashō's haiku was intended to amuse the reader by the clever borrowing of a phrase from an entirely different context.

Another of Bashō's earliest haiku that play with words written some time before 1664, focuses on a species of cherry tree called "old-lady cherry":

Ubazakura	The old-lady cherry
Saku ya rōgo no	Is blossoming, a remembrance
Omoiide	Of years ago.

There is a certain ambiguity in this verse which seems deliberate. On the surface it is about a cherry tree blossoming beautifully despite its old age. But the words "old-lady cherry" make it possible to interpret the poem as being about an old woman who still retains some of the loveliness of her youth. Furthermore, the phrase "a remembrance of years ago" has been taken from medieval Japanese drama, a nō play called *Sanemori* that tells of an old warrior gamely fighting his last battle among youthful soldiers. All this expands the meaning of the haiku, and the reader's main interest seems to lie in observing that expansion.

Relying equally on puns but less pedantic is a haiku Bashō probably composed a little later:

Akikaze no	The autumn wind
Yarido no kuchi ya	Through the opening of a sliding door—
Togarigoe	A piercing voice.

This contains two sets of word play. First, the Japanese word for "sliding" (*yari*, from *yaru*) also happens to mean "spear," which immediately invokes the association "to pierce." Secondly, the Japanese word for "opening" (*kuchi*) also denotes "mouth," thus bringing out a related word, "voice." The poem is a clever display of wit, if not much more.

Many of Bashō's earliest haiku are primarily intended to amuse, and the amusement is created by his skillful handling of the language. They express little of the poet's own sentiments, even when the occasion must have called for a display of genuine emotion. The following haiku, for instance, was written at the house of a person whose child had just died:

Shiorefusu ya	Drooping low
Yo wa sakasama no	In this topsy-turvy world,
Yuki no take	A bamboo plant under the snow.

Again the poem hinges on a pun: the Japanese word for "world" (*yo*) also has the meaning of "stalk." The "topsy-turvy world," then, assumes a double meaning: "the world that lets a child die before its parents" and "a bamboo stalk drooping its top to the ground." Furthermore, the last line is an inversion of the title of a nō play, *The Snow on the Bamboo (Take no Yuki)*, in which a mother mourns for her son who froze to death trying to remove snow from bamboos. These two sets of word play have certain merit: they unite two levels of meaning and create poetic ambiguity. Unfortunately they also have a demerit: the complexity and pedantry detract from the poem's lyricism. We cannot help thinking that an artless, straightforward lyric would have served its elegiac purpose more effectively.

Of course, young Bashō was simply following the conventions prevalent in his day. The so-called Teimon school of haikai, under whose influence Bashō began writing, advocated this sort of poetic technique. Inevitably, Bashō became more and more dissatisfied with the Teimon style as he grew older; thus in *The Seashell Game* of 1672 we find him moving away from it. One of the two haiku that bear his name in that book is:

Kite mo miyo	Come and look!
Jinbe ga haori	Wear a Jimbei robe
Hanagoromo	For your blossom viewing.

Word play is still used: in Japanese, "come" and "wear" are one word with two meanings. But the main interest of the poem lies in its first line, which seems to have been a phrase in vogue among young people at that time. "Come and look!" often appeared in the popular songs of the day. This note of contemporary town life is also echoed in "a Jimbei robe," which was a short, sleeveless robe worn by townsmen. The first two lines of the haiku, then, bring the poem's elegant subject, blossom-viewing, right down to earth. This indicates a new direction in Bashō's poetry, for his earlier haiku had always remained within the realm of elegant beauty and witty word play, frequently alluding to graceful court poetry and aristocratic nō dramas. Here in *The Seashell Game* he seems to be descending toward more earthy material, freely adopting popular phrases and colloquialisms.

II *Technique of Surprising Comparison: 1673–80*

The transition from refined wit to more earthy humor grew more apparent after Bashō came to Edo, and it was accelerated when the Danrin school of haikai, which arose in reaction to the Teimon school, began dominating the local poetic scene around 1675. The new school markedly expanded the scope of haikai in both theme and diction, extending it deeply into the life of the common people. Elegant subjects cherished by classical court poets were often parodied and ridiculed; word play and allusion were used not to show urbane wit but to provide a humorous contrast to some mundane subject.

One of Bashō's first poems after his arrival in Edo, cited below, clearly shows this transition. The haiku takes as its material one of the cherished subjects of classical Japanese poetry, a country woman pounding cloth on an autumn evening. In ancient times a court noble, traveling through the countryside, would often see a woman pounding cloth on a flat stone and would thereupon write a verse on the loneliness of travel. Parodying this poetic tradition, Bashō wrote a haiku:

Haritate ya	An acupuncturist
Kata ni tsuchi utsu	Hammering a needle into a shoulder—
Karakoromo	A robe cast off.

The Japanese word for "a robe cast off," *karakoromo,* also means "a Chinese-style robe," a garment often worn by ancient court nobles. The elegant picture of a high-ranking nobleman watching a country girl pound a Chinese-style robe to give it a fine finish, recedes into the background. Superimposed on it is the mundane view of an acupuncturist treating an overworked laborer at a disorderly tenement house.

A slightly later haiku alludes to a story that appears in *The Tales of Ise.* The story tells of a certain courtier who had a mistress. As the love affair was secret he could not enter her house openly; he had to sneak in over a crumbling section of the wall that guarded the house. An illustrious nobleman secretly in love with a charming lady whose family fortunes have declined—this is a fitting subject for a romantic story. But Bashō mocked it in a haiku:

Neko no tsuma	The cat's mistress
Hetsui no kuzure yori	Walks over a crumbled cooking stove
Kayoi keri	To a rendezvous.

The humor is enhanced by the fact that in the world of cats it is the female that goes to the male.

While ridiculing conventional poetic subjects, Bashō also wrote humorous haiku that do not rely on classical allusions. A good example is the following poem he produced on his westward journey in the summer of 1676, during which he passed by the snow-capped Mount Fuji. After arriving in his native province he was invited to an acquaintance's house on a hot day. During his visit Bashō, sending a breeze toward his host with a fan, recited:

Fuji no kaze ya	A wind from Mount Fuji
Ōgi ni nosete	Resting on the fan,
Edo miyage	My souvenir from Edo!

This is a witty poem, and nothing more. But it should be noted that the wit is not classical or contrived; it is simple, spontaneous, and lighthearted.

Another lighthearted and probably spontaneous haiku is one of his poems on moon-viewing. The reader should imagine Bashō and his friends aboard a small boat waiting for the harvest moon to rise. As befitted the occasion they were having some rice wine, and a round red wine cup was being washed in a large bowl made for that purpose. Suddenly a round red moon began to climb above the sea. Thereupon Bashō's poem:

Sōkai no	Waves on the blue ocean
Nami sake-kusashi	Smell of rice wine—
Kyō no tsuki	The moon of tonight.

The humor of the poem lies in its surprising comparison: the lovely moon shining over the sea is compared to a wine cup just taken out of a washing bowl. In earlier haiku Bashō brought together two unrelated objects by means of puns, as we have seen. Now he began to achieve this without depending on homonyms.

Using the technique of surprising comparison Bashō wrote another haiku, this time not so much to create humor as to generate a specifically poetic atmosphere. The poem is again about the harvest moon:

Ki o kirite	I fell a tree
Motokuchi miru ya	And gaze at the cut end—
Kyō no tsuki	The moon of tonight.

Here is a novel comparison of the round cut-end of a tree to the full moon, a comparison that produces surprise and humor. But the juxtaposition also yields a unique poetic atmosphere, for there seems to be something in common between the large full moon rising above the mountains and the freshly sawed section of a tree emitting a faint fragrance. They are both round, fresh-looking, and somehow suggestive of nature's hidden mystery.

As the years went by, Bashō came to write more and more serious poetry, freeing himself from the prevailing trend of humorous Danrin-style haiku. Some of his poems written in or shortly before 1680 exemplify his changing style admirably, for example this haiku about a spider:

Kumo nan to	Spider, I say!
Ne o nani to naku	In what voice do you chirp?
Aki no kaze	An autumn wind . . .

The humor lies in the colloquial tone of the first two lines, and in the unlikely reference to a spider's chirp. But the autumn wind reminds the reader of the solitude of a spider, which does not chirp for its mate but silently crouches in a web all by itself. There is definitely the image of a poet standing silent and alone in the autumn wind waiting for someone who may or may not come. Another haiku written about the same time has a similar comic overtone overlying deep solitude:

Gu anzuru ni	In my humble opinion
Meido mo kaku ya	Hades must be like this, too—
Aki no kure	Autumn evening.

"In my humble opinion," a cliché used by scholarly annotators of classics, is here employed for a comic purpose: Hades is too fantastic a subject to be explained away by a textual scholar. But this comic tone is immediately subdued in the third line, where the reader begins to wonder whether there is not something in common between Hades and an autumn evening.

In some of the haiku Bashō wrote around this time, the comic element is so much reduced that it seems almost nonexistent, as for instance, in the haiku entitled "The Moon on the Thirteenth of the Ninth Month":

Yoru hisokani	At night, quietly
Mushi wa gekka no	A worm in the moonlight
Kuri o ugatsu	Digs into a chestnut.

The whimsical connection of a chestnut and the moon of the thirteenth of the ninth month, traditionally called the Chestnut Moon, weighs little in the total meaning of the poem. Without the title to establish the connection, it is a fine poem catching the deadly quietness of an autumn night in the woods under a bright moon. Undoubtedly Bashō liked this sort of style and explored the possibilities further, until he came to write several haiku with no comic element whatsoever. For instance:

Izuku shigure	Where was the wintry shower?
Kasa o te ni sagete	With an umbrella in his hand
Kaeru sō	A monk returns.

The poem is almost purely descriptive. In the sky are thick gray clouds, and on the earth are bare trees and withered grass. It is a gloomy winter day, anticipating a shower at any moment. Here comes a Buddhist monk in a gray robe, returning to a small temple at the foot of the yonder hill. In his hand is an umbrella that looks wet; it must have been sprinkling where he had been visiting.

In addition to their somber overtone, the last two haiku clearly distinguish themselves from the earlier works in style as well. They are freer in form: in the original Japanese the chestnut poem consists of 6-7-6 syllable lines, and the umbrella poem of 6-8-5, straying considerably from the conventional 5-7-5 pattern. Furthermore, the orthography is rather unconventional; it approaches that of classical Chinese. For that matter, the umbrella poem in particular has a flavor of T'ang and Sung poetry in its subject matter. Apparently Bashō, weary of relying on wit and puns in the Japanese court tradition, had begun experimenting with the more somber and less artificial style of classical Chinese verse.

The best product of these experiments is a famous poem about a crow, with which it is said Bashō came into his own:

Kareeda ni	On a bare branch
Karasu no tomarikeri	A crow is perched—
Aki no kure	Autumn evening.

Again, the subject is very much like those of Chinese poetry and painting. The form is rather free, too, consisting of 5-10-5 syllable lines in the first version, and 5-9-5 in the final version. This haiku is superior to the last two poems we have seen, in that it contains neither calculated unexpectedness nor posed picturesqueness. It presents a scene that can be observed almost anywhere—or so the reader feels—so that the desolate atmosphere is not forced upon the reader. We might say the poem is objective and impersonal. When the umbrella poem asked "Where was the wintry shower?" the poet was present, but here he has almost vanished. This poem has probably been overpraised by later scholars who emphasize the importance of objectivity in haiku. But there is little doubt that it occupies a significant place as a milestone in Bashō's development.

III *In Search of Identity: 1681–85*

The first Bashō Hut was built in 1680, and the poet settled down there that winter. From around this time until 1685, when he wrote *The Records of a Weather-Exposed Skeleton* after his first significant journey, he went through a transitional period during which he sought to shake off the prevailing poetic mode and to establish a style of his own. As may be imagined, he experimented with various styles, most of which had their roots in his earlier poetry. Perhaps we can classify these transitional styles in three categories. First, he continued to absorb and assimilate the language of classical Chinese poetry, the culmination of which was *Shriveled Chestnuts*. Secondly, he cultivated his earlier technique of surprising comparison, which resulted in several excellent haiku. And thirdly, he went on writing descriptive, objective haiku; some of the poems in *The Records of a Weather-Exposed Skeleton* are fine examples of this style. We shall examine several examples from each of these categories.

The haiku written under the influence of Chinese verse show the same characteristics as those of the earlier period: they are liberal in syllable pattern, use a pseudo-Chinese orthography, and create a somber, lonely mood. One change, however, is that Bashō wrote these haiku out of his own personal experience. A good example is one of the earliest haiku he wrote after moving into the Bashō Hut:

Ro no koe nami o utte	The sound of an oar beating the waves
Harawata kōru	Chills my bowels through
Yo ya namida	And I weep in the night.

The syllable pattern is 10-7-5. "The sound of an oar" and "chills my bowels through" are clichés in classical Chinese poetry. The hyperbolic style poeticizing loneliness is also from T'ang verse; in fact, Bashō's headnote to the haiku refers to a poem by Tu Fu. Yet the headnote also makes clear that the haiku is intended to embody a cold winter night as felt by the poet in his modest hut near the river. The elements of Chinese verse are made to serve his prime purpose: to present his own feelings.

Chinese elements are more closely integrated with his personal experience in the following haiku, which appears in *Shriveled Chestnuts*. It has a short headnote, "At this modest hut I buy water," meaning that Bashō had to buy water and keep it in a container—his district produced no good water. The haiku was written in winter.

Kōri nigaku	Ice tastes bitter
Enso ga nodo o	In the mouth of a sewer rat
Uruoseri	Quenching his thirst.

The reference is to a passage in a Taoist classic *Chuang-tzu*, which says that a sewer rat's thirst is easily quenched with a tiny drink from a large river. The passage, intended to strike home the moral that one can attain happiness only by living within one's means, does not come to the foreground of Bashō's poem. In fact, the haiku is not at all didactic; all it has borrowed from *Chuang-tzu* is the image of a rat taking a drink of water. On a cold night Bashō felt thirsty and wanted a drink of water. He went to the kitchen of his modest hut and, finding the water frozen, broke off a piece of ice and put it into his mouth. It was so cold that it tasted bitter, and Bashō momentarily thought of *Chuang-tzu's* dirty rat living in a sewer.

Bashō's finest poems in this period belong to the second category, where two things not ordinarily associated with each other are brought together by the poet's imagination. We have already seen the genesis of this feature: the full moon and a round wine cup, for instance, were associated in a haiku to produce surprise. Bashō now began to juxtapose two disparate objects not so much for the shock effect as to create a specific mood or sensation which could not otherwise be evoked. Fine examples of this appear in *The Records of a Weather-Exposed Skeleton*. For example:

Akebono ya	In the twilight of dawn
Shirauo shiroki	A whitefish, with an inch
Koto issun	Of whiteness.

This whitefish is a kind of icefish that lives in Japanese lakes. A slender fish about two inches long, it looks almost transparent in the water but turns silvery white when taken out. The traveling poet woke at dawn one day and went to the lakeshore, where local fishermen were pulling in their net. Among various kinds of fish caught in the net, a young whitefish was flopping about. In the twilight of dawn, which seemed to extend into an infinite distance over the lake, its whiteness was beautifully clear and definite. Much of the beauty of the poem lies in this unique combination of the twilight and the whitefish.

If this poem embodies delicate picturesque beauty, the following haiku, which uses a similar method of combining, presents a more violent atmosphere. Bashō was at Ise, and visited one of the Grand Shinto Shrines deep in the cedar woods:

Misoka tsuki nashi	The last night of the month, no moon:
Chitose no sugi o	Thousand-year-old cedars
Daku arashi	Besieged by a storm.

The black of night on the thirtieth of a lunar month, ancient cedar trees with their dark green needles, and the stormy gusts that blow through them with a roar, are all combined to produce a feeling of being in the primitive, rugged universe before the birth of man, the kind of universe inhabited only by ancient Shinto gods.

Totally different in tone but using a similar method is the following poem, also composed during his journey of 1684. This time Bashō stopped for lunch at a teashop on the roadside:

Tsutsuji ikete	Azaleas in a bucket
Sono kage ni hidara	And in their shade, a woman
Saku onna	Tearing up a dried codfiish.

Azaleas are wild in western Japan, and a traveler sees them blooming everywhere along mountain roads in late spring. In this haiku long branches of azalea blossoms are casually put in a bucket in a corner of the teashop, and under them the proprietress is preparing a codfish for the customer. Azalea blossoms and a codfish, thus brought together, produce an atmosphere of modest and peaceful rusticity. In fact the reader can almost picture the proprietress: she must be somewhat over thirty, married and with children, her hands hardened with housework yet still retaining some of the charm of her youth.

In these three poems, Bashō juxtaposed two or more visual images. In the following two haiku he combined two sensory perceptions, thereby creating a novel atmosphere:

Ran no ka ya	The fragrant orchid:
Chō no tsubasa ni	Into a butterfly's wings
Takimono su	It breathes the incense.

This poem, unusually colorful for Bashō, derives its effect from the merging of a scent with a visual image. The effect is heightened by the use of Sino-Japanese readings of some of the words in the poem, such as *ran* (orchid), *ka* (fragrance), and *chō* (butterfly). More typical is:

Kogarashi ya	A wintry gust
Take ni kakurete	Disappears amid the bamboos
Shizumarinu	And subsides to a calm.

Here a sense of motion is combined with visual scenery. In both instances there is a delicate harmony between two different senses. The strong aroma of an orchid goes well with the colorful wings of a butterfly, and a chilling gust of wind is fitting for a bamboo plant with its lean stalk and pointed leaves.

The merging of different senses, when carried further, will produce synesthesia. That is exactly the case in the next haiku written by Bashō in the same period:

Umi kurete	The sea darkens
Kamo no koe	And a wild duck's call
Honokani shiroshi	Is faintly white.

The wild duck's call, faintly heard in the offing as dusk fell, could not be described in any way other than by the color white. It evokes in the reader a vision of the vast, dim darkness falling over the ocean, and a lonely feeling of the poet on the shore gazing into the darkness. This verse can be said to have reached the peak level of Bashō's poetry.

The third type of haiku written in this period is an extension of the earlier line that culminated in the crow poem. The poems show neither Chinese elements nor striking juxtapositions of two objects or senses; they are plain in setting, straightforward in structure, regular in syllable pattern, and lucid in diction. In fact, they sometimes look so ordinary that one starts wondering where their real meaning lies. The truth is that these poems are intentionally plain and ambiguous. They present an experience without the poet's commentary on it, because the poet wants the reader to go through it himself. How to interpret this experience is up to the individual reader.

A good example of this is a famous poem with the headnote "On Horseback":

Michinobe no	Blooming by the lane
Mukuge wa uma ni	A rose mallow—and it has been
Kuwarekeri	Devoured by the horse!

All the poem says is that a flower blooming by the lane was eaten by a horse. Scholars have tried to interpret the poem in widely differing ways. Some have said, for instance, that the haiku embodies the Buddhist idea of life's mutability. Others have claimed that it preaches the virtue (and benefit) of modesty and unobtrusiveness. A third group of readers have interpreted it simply as a poem sketching an actual occurrence. In view of Bashō's headnote, the third interpretation seems to be closest to its original intention. But what is not often realized is that the poet is not trying to state his reaction to the little incident. Bashō wants each reader to go on horseback along a country lane and to watch the horse eat a rose mallow. How to interpret the experience—Bashō has left that to the reader.

An equally well-known haiku, written a little later, is based on Bashō's experience during the same trip:

Yamaji kite	Along the mountain road
Nani yara yukashi	Somehow it tugs at my heart:
Sumiregusa	A wild violet.

The poem looks alomst frivolous: it simply presents a violet blooming alongside a mountain road. The poet does comment this time—"somehow it tugs at my heart"—but the comment is general and vague. Again Bashō wants us to take part in his experience: he expects us to travel over lonely, tiresome mountain road and to suddenly discover a tiny violet at the roadside. The loveliness of the purple that brightens a corner of the desolate scene, the familiar feeling it calls to mind as one of the flowers predominant in childhood memories, the warmth of its womanly contours which dissipate the traveler's solitude for a moment—all this and probably more is implied in the words "somehow it tugs at my heart." The sensation Bashō felt at that moment was so all-inclusive that more specific words would have unduly limited its range. So what Bashō did was make a very general comment, hoping we would be able to relive his experience.

Another haiku so plainly descriptive as to create ambiguity is:

Chō no tobu	A butterfly flits
Bakari nonaka no	All alone—and on the field,
Hikage kana	A shadow in the sunlight.

This is susceptible of various allegorical and didactic interpretations. But the simple truth seems to be that Bashō saw a butterfly flitting about over a field in the bright sunlight and transformed his immediate sensation into a poem before it began to move in any intellectual or moral direction. The reader is expected to experience that preintellectual and premoral sensation.

All in all, we see Bashō in this period gradually broadening the scope of his haiku by cultivating different poetic techniques. His haiku began to distinguish themselves more clearly from those of other poets, who were still writing in older styles. Of factors that made it possible for him to do this, one is especially noteworthy. Bashō had now come to write more and more haiku deriving from his own experience rather than from classical Chinese and Japanese literature. He started out with an emotion or pre-emotion that arose from an experience in his life, and this made it necessary for him to sacrifice such elements as wit, word play, grace, shock effect, or anything else foreign to that pre-emotion. For Bashō, poetry was no longer recreational; it was creative in the true sense of the word.

IV *Manifestations of Sabi: 1686-91*

The period from 1686 to 1691 can be considered the peak years of Bashō's creative activities, producing *A Visit to the Kashima Shrine, The Records of a Travel-Worn Satchel, A Visit to Sarashina Village, The Narrow Road to the Deep North, The Saga*

Diary, and *The Monkey's Cloak.* Specifically in the haiku, Bashō was now a master craftsman, using numerous techniques with freedom and ease. And more important, he established a distinctive style. He might borrow from Chinese verse, juxtapose two disparate objects, create ambiguity of meaning, or rely on any number of other methods, and yet his poems always had something uniquely his own. This unique quality can be explained by applying the idea of sabi; many of the poems characteristic of Bashō's work in this period have the quality of sabi. We must remember, however, that sabi is a principle that manifests itself in a number of ways and that Bashō exploited all of them. For this reason the haiku of this period, despite their common quality of sabi, encompass a range just as wide as those of any other period.

The noun *sabi* originally derived from an adjective, *sabishi,* which meant "lonely" or "solitary," usually describing a person in want of company. Bashō, however, seems to have used it in a more specific sense. The following is one of several haiku that contain the word *sabishi* in its substantive form:

Sabishisa ya	Loneliness—
Kugi ni kaketaru	Hanging from a nail,
Kirigirisu	A cricket.

According to the note of someone who was with Bashō when he wrote this poem, he was staying at a small cottage near Lake Biwa in the autumn of 1691. Late one night, still lying awake, he heard the feeble chirp of a cricket kept in a cage hanging from a nail on the wall. The "loneliness" in this haiku, then, is that expressed in a cricket's faint but serene chirp fading into the vast darkness of late autumn night. A similar use of "loneliness" is observed in a haiku written two years earlier:

Sabishisa ya	Loneliness—
Iwa ni shimikomu	Sinking into the rocks,
Semi no koe	A cicada's cry.

Bashō was visiting an ancient Buddhist temple on a remote rocky mountain and heard a cicada's cry among ancient pine and oak trees, a long-sustained chirp "sinking" into the impenetrable rocks.

It is interesting to note that there remains what appears to be a different draft of each of these poems:

Shizukasa ya *E kakaru kabe no* *Kirigirisu*	Quietness– On the wall, where a picture hangs, A cricket.
Shizukasa ya *Iwa ni shimiiru* *Semi no koe*	Quietness– Sinking into the rocks, A citada's cry.

Certainly it is more than a coincidence that the word "quietness" is used in place of "loneliness" in both poems. Bashō conceived loneliness to be very close to quietness. In his usage, then, loneliness does not just mean that one is alone and in need of company; it has more to do with a particular atmosphere arising from a scene or moment that need not involve a human being. In these two poems there is no man; there are only a cricket and a cicada. The "lonely" or "quiet" atmosphere is created when such a tiny living thing fulfils its destiny within the vast expanse of the universe. The fragile life of a little creature merging into the immense power of nature, like the cricket's chirp fading into the autumn night or the cicada's cry sinking into the rocks, seems to lie at the root of Bashō's concept of loneliness and of sabi. To realize that all living things are evanescent is sad, but when one sees a tiny creature enduring that sadness and fulfilling its destiny one is struck with a sublime feeling. The haiku most characteristic of Bashō in this period seem to point toward this sublime feeling.

Needless to say, a haiku can create the atmosphere of sabi without actually using the words lonely or loneliness. Indeed, these words might unduly restrict the reader's imagination. The following haiku by Bashō, written between 1686 and 1691, all seem to have the implication of sabi. Characteristically, each centers on the merging of the temporal into the eternal, of the mutable into the indestructible, of the tiny and finite into the vast and infinite, out of which emerges a primeval lonely feeling shared by all things in this world.

Hototogisu *Kieyuku kata ya* *Shima hitotsu*	A cuckoo– Far out where it disappears, A lone island.
Horo horo to *Yamabuki chiru ka* *Taki no oto*	Quietly, quietly, Yellow mountain roses fall– Sound of the rapids.
Fuyu-niwa ya *Tsuki mo ito naru* *Mushi no gin*	Above a wintry garden The moon thins to a thread: Insect's singing.
Koe sumite *Hokuto ni hibiku* *Kinuta kana*	The sound is clear And reaches the Big Dipper: Someone pounding cloth.
Furuike ya *Kawazu tobikomu* *Mizu no oto*	The old pond– A frog leaps in, And a splash.

These poems are somewhat ambiguous because the poet has not specified his response to the experience; the last, in particular, has invited an enormous number of interpretations through the centuries. Yet basic to them all seems to be an internal comparison, a comparison between the finite and the infinite which are brought together in one experience, which is the poem. Ambiguity arises when one tries to rationalize that experience in different ways. How does one explain the relationship between the pond that has been there for centuries and a tiny splash that disappears in a moment, between the eternal Big Dipper and the brief sound of cloth being pounded, or between the incessant sound of the rapids and the falling petals of yellow mountain roses? Different people will give different answers, though they will all experience the same sort of "loneliness" when they try to give explanations. It seems that Bashō was more concerned with the "loneliness" than with the answers.

In some of his haiku Bashō gives only half of the comparison, leaving the other half unsaid. In such poems the infinity, immensity, strength, or indifference of the universe prevails, and the reader has the feeling of being overpowered, absorbed, or dissolved. Here are a few examples:

Araumi ya *Sado ni yokotau* *Amanogawa*	The rough sea— Extending toward Sado Isle, The Milky Way.
Samidare o *Atsumete hayashi* *Mogami-gawa*	Gathering the rains Of summer, how swiftly flows The Mogami River!
Atsuki hi o *Umi ni iretari* *Mogami-gawa*	The scorching sun Flows into the ocean With the Mogami River.
Fukitobasu *Ishi wa asama no* *Nowaki kana*	Blowing the gravel Off the rocks of Mount Asama, An autumn gale.
Kogarashi ni *Iwa fukitogaru* *Sugima kana*	Against the wintry gust How sharp are the rocks Amid the cedars!
Ishiyama no *Ishi yori shiroshi* *Aki no kaze*	On the Stone Mountain, It is whiter than the stones: Autumnal wind.

In these poems there is hardly a trace of human life; only the primitive universe as it has been for eons. How Bashō felt when confronted with that reality, he does not say. He wants the reader himself to face the vastness of the galaxy, the swiftness of the Mogami River, or the forcefulness of the Asama gale.

A little less impersonal, some poems allow a man to come in and face the powerful manifestations of the inanimate universe. Many of the poems were written in winter, when this power is at its harshest:

Kame waruru *Yoru no kōri no* *Nezame kana*	The sound of a water jar Cracking on this icy night As I lie awake.

Fuyu no hi ya
Bajō ni kōru
Kagebōshi

The winter sun—
Frozen on the horse,
My shadow.

Negi shiroku
Araitatetaru
Samusa kana

A pile of leeks lie
Newly washed white:
How cold it is!

Ikameshiki
Oto ya arare no
Hinoki-gasa

How harsh it sounds!
The spattering of the hail
On my traveling hat.

The coldness that emanates from these poems is not really that of wintry temperature, but has more to do with some essential quality of the universe we live in. It seems to approach "loneliness," for the man in these haiku is suddenly awake to the hidden power of the universe that manifests itself in the human world with no concern for the welfare of its inhabitants. The awakening makes him feel insignificant, lonely, and "cold."

In what way can man overcome, or at least bear with, this icy loneliness? The answer Bashō arrived at seems to have derived from his observation of nature, especially of trees, plants, and grass, which of all living things have the least capacity to protect themselves from the elements. They simply endure what is given to them, and thereby maintain an equilibrium. They never attempt to be other than themselves; they undeviatingly follow their destiny to the end. The following poems seem to suggest Bashō's move in this direction:

Hatsuyuki ya
Suisen no ha no
Tawamu made

The first snow—
Daffodil leaves bend
Under the weight.

Yasenagara
Warinaki kiku no
Tsubomi kana

Emaciated,
How punctually the chrysanthemum
Begins to bud!

Yoku mireba
Nazuna hana saku
Kakine kana

Looking closely, I see
A shepherd's purse blooming
Under the hedge.

Okiagaru	As they begin to rise again
Kiku honoka nari	Chrysanthemums faintly smell,
Mizu no ato	After the flooding rain.

Here we see small vegetable life placed under harsh conditions. It has to suffer, without having done any wrong to anything or anyone. Nevertheless it accepts its fate with no bitterness; it silently goes on to fulfil its preordained functions.

Furthermore, Bashō apparently believed in the idea that things of the vegetable and mineral worlds cope with loneliness by communicating with each other. It seemed to him that they know they all share in the life of the universe, as suggested in the following:

Hi no michi ya	Toward the sun's path
Aoi katamuku	Hollyhock flowers turning
Satsuki-ame	In the rains of summer.
Kane kiete	After the chimes fade
Hana no ka wa tsuku	Cherry fragrance continues:
Yūbe kana	Evening dusk.
Kareshiba ya	On the withered grass
Yaya kagerō no	Shimmering heat waves rise
Ichinisun	One or two inches high.
Suisen ya	The daffodils
Shiroki shōji no	And the white paper screen
Tomoutsuri	Reflecting one another's color.

In each of these poems there is an implied communication: between the sun and the hollyhock, between the chimes and the scent of cherry blossoms, between the grass and the air, and between the daffodils and the white screen. Bashō's old method of bringing together two disparate objects is revitalized to exemplify this hidden interrelatedness.

In order to overcome loneliness, then, man should follow the ways of nature; he should try to communicate with the vegetable and mineral worlds. He should be able to do so, for within himself lies something that is common to all things. With this assumption Bashō goes on to sing of the rare, precious moments of communication between man and nature:

Asacha nomu	A monk sipping
Sō shizukanari	His morning tea, and it is quiet—
Kiku no hana	Chrysanthemum flowers.
Kutabirete	Weary from travel
Yado karu koro ya	I seek a lodging for the night—
Fuji no hana	Wistaria flowers.
Te o uteba	I clap my hands
Kodama ni akuru	And with the echoes, the day begins to dawn—
Natsu no tsuki	The summer moon.
Kagerō no	Heat waves
Waga kata ni tatsu	Shimmer on the shoulders
Kamiko kana	Of my paper robe.

Chrysanthemums, Bashō felt, have a unique tranquillity possessed also by a Zen monk sipping his morning tea in the cell. A tired traveler who saw some purple wistaria dangling from a trellis in the evening dusk found a harmony between the flowers and the weariness of his mind and body. The man who clapped his hands felt as if the universe responded, and the man in a paper robe felt at one with all the things around him that were wavering in the heat. These poems, even the one about the tired traveler, exhibit no trace of loneliness.

In those rare moments when Bashō witnessed a happy communication between man and nature, he wrote some lighthearted, even humorous poems. Here is an instance:

Hitotsuya ni	Under the same roof
Yūjo mo netari	Courtesans, too, are asleep—
Hagi to tsuki	Bush clover and the moon.

Bush clover blooming in the garden and the autumn moon shining in the sky are thousands of miles apart, yet they come together and seem to become companions. Watching the scene, Bashō is led to perceive a similar bond between a traveling poet in a gray robe and two pretty courtesans who happened to lodge at the same inn. Another haiku in the same category is also about bush clover:

Nurete yuku	Drenched passersby:
Hito mo okashi ya	They too are beautiful–
Ame no hagi	Bush clover in the rain.

The poem implies a relationship between drenched men and bush clover, and when that relationship is discovered even ordinary people are seen to be as beautiful as the flowers. The rain, which falls on all things, reveals this. Both poems emit a gleam of humor: the first conjures up the incongruous picture of an ascetic poet sleeping in the same house as the courtesans, and in the second the reader knows that the passersby did not enjoy being drenched with rain.

The humor is more apparent in the next three haiku. The first was composed one night at a firefly-viewing party on the river:

Hotaru-mi ya	Firefly viewing–
Sendō yōte	The steersman is drunk
Obotsukana	And how unsteady the boat!

Between the unsteady boat on the dark river and little fireflies slowly flitting about emitting feeble bursts of light, there undoubtedly seems to be a relationship. The next haiku was written one winter day when there were flashes of lightning, a warning of a coming snowfall:

Yuki o matsu	Waiting for the snow,
Jōgo no kao ya	Wine lovers' faces–
Inabikari	A flash of lightning.

The wine lovers are of course poets, who eagerly wait for the snow (their favorite poetic subject) and for a snow-viewing party (where wine will be served). That eager expectation is heightened by the lightning that heralds the snowfall. The third is unlike the first two in that it has nothing to do with wine:

Kogarashi ya	A wintry gust—
Hōbare itamu	His cheeks painfully swollen,
Hito no kao	Face of a man.

This poem is based on the poet's discovery of a relationship between the chilling gusts of winter and the face of a person with mumps—material that is scarcely humorous in itself. And yet the unexpected juxtaposition, the objectivity of presentation, and the image of a distorted face combine to coax a smile from the reader.

Humor was not new in Bashō s poetry; as we have seen, he used it even as an amateur versifier. But its nature has completely changed. In the early days laughter was generated by means of puns and word play, or of interesting ways of alluding to passages from the classics. A little later Bashō introduced the technique of surprising comparison, but by and large he used it only to obtain a shock effect. In these later poems the belief that all things are mutually communicable, that a person can become at one with other creations of nature, seems to underlie the humor. This attitude was to evolve into the concept of "lightness." In fact, one of the few haiku to which Bashō is said to have applied the term "lightness" was written in this period, and indeed it has much in common with the poems we have just cited. The haiku, written in the spring of 1690, is:

Ki no moto ni	Under the trees
Shiru mo namasu mo	Soup, fish salad, and everywhere
Sakura kana	Cherry blossoms.

It is the scene of a picnic under cherry trees in bloom, and petals fall on people, picnic dishes, rice wine—everything that happens to be there. Here there is an implication of nature benignly enveloping all things, including man, within itself. All man has to do is give himself up to this embrace. In Bashō's view, this is the way for man to cope with the depressing isolation that threatens him.

V *Last Phase: 1692–94*

The haiku of Bashō's last three years show him moving from the world of nature to the world of man. In actual life, he returned to Edo in the winter of 1691 and began to live more gregariously. A famed poet, he now associated with many nonpoets; he also had some relatives to look after. The leisurely life he had enjoyed at the Unreal Hut and the House of Fallen Persimmons was no longer possible, and communication with nature, which had formerly helped to dissolve his loneliness, could seldom be attained in the hustle and bustle of urban life. The principle of sabi, at which he had arrived after a long search, did not seem to be universally valid.

It is no wonder that some of the haiku of this period show bitterness, frustration, and even despair to an unusual degree. We have already seen his bitter cynicism:

Toshidoshi ya	Year after year
Saru ni kisetaru	On the monkey's face,
Saru no men	A monkey's mask.

We have also noted that he closed his gate and shut out all visitors with the haiku:

Asagao ya	The morning-glory–
Hiru wa jō orosu	In the daytime, a bolt is fastened
Mon no kaki	On the frontyard gate.

He wanted to be left alone; he wanted to have only the morning-glory for his friend. But even its innocent beauty failed to provide consolation:

Asagao ya	The morning-glory–
Kore mo mata waga	That, too, now turns out
Tomo narazu	Not to be my friend.

The haiku reveals a deep solitude that approaches nihilism.

Three of Bashō's most famous poems written in this period reflect such loneliness, not of the kind that brings man closer to the heart of nature, but of the kind that deepens his feelings of alienation. The first haiku, produced about the time he closed the gate, reads:

Mono ieba	Whenever I speak out
Kuchibiru samushi	My lips are chilled—
Aki no kaze	Autumnal wind.

The poem expresses bitter frustration with the lack of communication among individuals. Probably Bashō had been talking with someone who did not understand or misunderstood what he said; now recalling the incident in his bitter memory as he walked alone in the autumn wind, he regretted that he had even spoken. Another haiku that embodies deep frustration and resulting solitude is:

Kono michi ya	The road here—
Yuku hito nashi ni	No traveler comes along
Aki no kure	This autumn evening.

The road in the poem is at once literal and symbolic. And we should remember that this was written when Bashō was at the peak of his fame, surrounded by countless followers. The third haiku was composed less than a fortnight before his death:

Aki fukaki	Autumn deepens—
Tonari wa nani o	The man next door, what
Suru hito zo	Does he do for a living?

Again Bashō laments the isolation of the individual. Even next door neighbors do not know each other; their lives are completely separate. If a person does not even know what his next-door neighbor does for living, how can he be expected to understand other people's inner thoughts?

Indifference and cruelty are not limited to human life; they exist in nature also. Several of Bashō's late haiku about nature are strikingly devoid of warmth, loveliness, and quietude. Intercommunication is there, but it is at the level of ugliness, sickness, and cruelty. For instance:

Samidare ya — The rainy season—
Kaiko wazurau — The silkworms are ailing
Kuwa no hata — In the mulberry field.

Certainly there is a harmony between the gloomy rain of early summer and the white, ailing silkworms abandoned in a field, but the atmosphere it generates is unlike that of a usual Bashō poem. Here is another haiku that is unpleasantly different:

Namagusashi — How fishy they smell!
Konagi ga ue no — On a waterweed,
Hae no wata — Dace entrails.

The poem successfully conveys the feeling of a disgustingly hot and humid day, combining the sliminess of a waterweed and the repellent smell of a dead dace with its intestines exposed. The technique is unmistakably Bashō's, but it is employed to create a disagreeable feeling. More straightforward in expressing the cruelty and ugliness of life is:

Ikinagara — Still alive,
Hitotsu ni kōru — They are frozen in one lump:
Namako kana — Sea slugs.

The deep coldness of this poem is all the more striking because slippery sea slugs were usually a comic subject in the Japanese literary tradition.

We have so far concentrated on poems that seem to reflect Bashō's agony and despair in his last years; but all this while Bashō was trying to dispel the agony and overcome the despair. As can be imagined, his effort was directed toward the attainment of "lightness," toward the acceptance of all things as they are. He found it impossible to escape from the world of men, for he himself was a man; the only alternative was to bear with the imperfections of human nature and to smile them away. An interesting haiku that shows this attitude is:

Nusubito ni — There was a night, too,
Ōta yo mo ari — When a robber visited my home—
Toshi no kure — The year end.

Here the poet, looking back over the year as it comes to an end, is not bitter toward the robber who stole things from his home. Rather, he seems to be recalling the incident with a smile, as the word "visited" suggests. It looks as if he had come to a state of mind where he could accept that the world of men abounds with thieves and robbers. Another interesting haiku that suggests this frame of mind is:

Niwa hakite	While sweeping the garden
Yuki o wasururu	It forgets about the snow:
Hahaki kana	The broom.

According to the headnote, the man in the poem holding a broom and sweeping the snow out of the garden is a noted Chinese Zen monk. While sweeping the snow, he has forgotten about the snow. This seems to be the point Bashō was trying to reach; he wished to forget the mire while living amid the mire.

Understandably, Bashō wrote more and more poems about the world of men toward the end of his life. Instead of escaping into nature, he tried to live among men. If he had moments of despair, he also had moments when he could contemplate human reality with a smile. Here is a haiku that records one of his happier moments:

Ika-uri no	The squid-seller's voice
Koe magirawashi	Is indistinguishable
Hototogisu	From the cuckoo's!

The poet lives amid the noises of the town, where various hawkers cry their wares. He has been trying to listen to the poetic song of a cuckoo, when he hears a squid-seller calling and finds it impossible to distinguish his cry from the cuckoo's. Bashō, however, is not irritated; rather, he is amused. Another instance that shows Bashō accepting heterogeneities of human life is:

Mononofu no	Samurai gathering–
Daikon nigaki	Their chat has the pungent taste
Hanashi kana	Of horse radish.

Here the poet, who was used to carefree chats among ordinary townsmen, was invited to join a group from the ruling warrior class and found that their conversation, reflecting their neo-Confucian upbringing, was somewhat rigorous and dignified even on this informal occasion. But Bashō did not alienate himself from the group; he chose to enjoy that rather stiff atmosphere, humorously comparing it to the taste of a radish.

Bashō's increased interest in ordinary people's lives made it possible for him to write haiku that in effect condense a short story. A good example is:

Susuhaki wa	The Year-End Cleaning–
Ono ga tana tsuru	Hanging a shelf in his own house,
Daiku kana	A carpenter.

Few men like their family life to be invaded by their professional concerns; they want their homes reserved for relaxation, a place where they can completely forget their business. Thus a gardener often neglects his own garden; a professional cook seldom prepares a dinner at home; and a carpenter, who can build a whole house if he wants to, ignores repeated pleas from his wife to hang a small shelf on the wall for her. But today is the thirteenth of the twelfth month, traditionally the day of housecleaning in preparation for the New Year, and this carpenter has taken a day off to help his wife tidy the house. Taking this opportunity, he is at long last hanging a shelf for his wife, probably with a grin on his face. A passerby, noticing the rare occasion, also cannot help but smile. The haiku shows no trace of Bashō the recluse.

It does not follow, however, that Bashō practically gave up writing haiku about nature. On the contrary, the majority of the haiku of this last period are still about nature. Yet it seems to be undeniable that many of those nature poems have come to show a trace of human life, and that few embody the poet's longing for the primeval, prehuman world. The coldness that permeated many of his earlier poems has been replaced by the warmth of "lightness." When Bashō brings together two disparate objects to create a uniquely harmonious atmosphere, one of them is more often than not related to human life, to *ordinary* human life. For instance, here are two haiku on chrysanthemums:

Kiku no hana	Chrysanthemum flowers
Saku ya ishiya no	Bloom—amid the stones
Ishi no ai	In a stone dealer's yard.

Kiku no ka ya	Chrysanthemums' scent—
Niwa ni kiretaru	In the garden, the worn-out
Kutsu no soko	Shoe sole.

The first poem capitalizes on a strange bond between the refreshing loveliness of chrysanthemums and the cold ruggedness of unpolished stones; this is typical of Bashō's method of juxtaposition between two objects of nature. Yet the setting is the yard of a stone dealer near a busy dock in Edo. The second poem is set in a lovely garden filled with the scent of chysanthemums. But Bashō has placed in its very center the sole of an old shoe, suggesting the owner's carefree way of life. In both cases beauty has been found when the realm of nature is expanded to include men and their daily lives.

In this sense it could be said that Bashō's poetic world was greatest in scope in those last years. All things, human and nonhuman, are included in his haiku. He could take a most unlikely object and make it the subject of his poem. The best-known example of this is:

Uguisu ya	A bush warbler—
Mochi ni fun suru	It lets its droppings fall on the rice cake
En no saki	At the end of the veranda.

This is a beautiful spring scene, in which the poet quietly watches a bush warbler on his veranda in the warm sunshine. Another haiku, describing an autumn scene, is exquisitely beautiful:

Mikazuki ni	Under the crescent moon
Chi wa oboro nari	The earth looms hazily—
Soba no hana	Buckwheat flowers.

The dim crescent moon, the dusky earth in the haze, and innumerable white flowers blanketing the spacious farm are harmoniously blended in a manner very much like that of his poetry of sabi. The difference is that buckwheat flowers are commonplace in Japan and not especially beautiful; moreover, buckwheat is the main ingredient of one of the plainest foods, noodles. Another fine poem that approaches sabi with a difference is the well-known haiku:

Kiku no ka ya	Chrysanthemums' scent—
Nara ni wa furuki	In the old town of Nara,
Hotoke-tachi	Many ancient Buddhas.

Nara was the national capital centuries ago, when Buddhism arrived in Japan and brought with it the flourishing cultures of India and China. Now the city is no longer the capital, and Buddhism is past its prime, too. Yet Nara's temples still contain wooden images of Buddha, which have sat there quietly through the centuries. The ancient world those Buddhas watched with their merciful eyes is somehow present in the elegant, noble fragrance of chrysanthemums that pervades the air of Nara. Inhaling that fragrance, one feels as if the ancient images were alive and breathing. It is significant that the poem says "Buddhas" and not "Buddhist images"; they were felt to be living in Nara, in the world of men.

In the last years of his life, then, Bashō was making an effort to modify his idea of sabi, if not to transform it. Sabi had suggested that man turn to primitive nature and submerge himself in the vegetable and mineral worlds and thus dissolve his ego, the source of all tormenting desires. Now Bashō was trying to devise a way in which man could remain in the mundane world and still attain peace of mind. His solution was "lightness," an attitude by which man accepts all things as they come, like the poet-recluse who could smile away an encounter with a robber, or the Zen monk who forgot about the snow while sweeping away the snow. Was Bashō really successful in this effort? Did he actually overcome that almost misanthropic despair suggested in some of his haiku?

We shall never be given a definitive answer. All we can do is take a look at several verses written in the last days of his life to see what feelings they embody. Here is a haiku Bashō wrote a fortnight before his death:

Shiragiku no	A white chrysanthemum—
Me ni tatete miru	However intently I gaze,
Chiri mo nashi	Not a speck of dust.

This is a lovely poem. Bashō was looking at a white chrysanthemum at the house of some friends during a gathering, but the haiku creates a feeling that for Bashō at that moment nothing existed but the flower's pure whiteness. It seems to be the sort of poem that could not be written in the absence of serenity.

The following evening Bashō joined a group of poets, each of whom composed a haiku on the theme of love. Bashō's was entitled "Accompanying a Handsome Youth under the Moon":

Tsuki sumu ya	How serene the moon!
Kitsune kowagaru	I escort a handsome youth
Chigo no tomo	Frightened by a fox's howl.

The scene is created from Bashō's imagination. Late at night a young catamite is walking home along a road that passes through the woods. The moon is bright in the sky, but in the woods it is dark, and from the darkness comes a fox's uncanny howl, frightening the boy. The universe is beautiful under the serene moon, but it is also pregnant with weird mysteries that frighten the young and inexperienced. It may not be possible for Bashō to dispel the boy's fear completely, but at least he can keep him company.

During the thirteen days that remained, Bashō wrote two more haiku. The first, probably composed shortly after the fox poem, is the haiku we have seen in which Bashō asks what his next-door neighbor does for living. It has an implication of man's infinite solitude, a deep pessimism about the communicability of ideas among individuals. This certainly lacks the serenity and tenderness of the chrysanthemum poem and the fox poem. Then came Bashō's last poem, written just four days before his death:

Tabi ni yande	On a journey, ailing—
Yume wa kareno o	My dreams roam about
Kakemeguru	Over a withered moor.

This poem too points in a direction quite distant from a pure white chrysanthemum or the serenely shining moon. Bashō did know this world was a withered moor, but he had to keep wandering in search of a place of rest. Neither sabi nor "lightness" could completely set his mind at ease. Restlessly he roamed around, and in the course of doing so he created a number of poems that tell us the successes and failures of his search.

CHAPTER 3

The Renku

THE RENKU is a unique type of poem with multiple authorship. It normally consists of thirty-six, fifty, or one hundred verses (or stanzas) contributed by a "team" of poets. Composing a renku is very much like a group game; in point of fact, amusement is the prime motivation of an ordinary renku-writing gathering. We can imagine, for instance, one of the participants coming up with an exquisitely beautiful verse or with an immensely humorous one, and the rest of the group sighing in admiration or bursting into laughter. The primary advantage of the renku as a verse form is that it is possible to attain a scope and variety that ordinarily lie outside the capacity of a single poet.

Yet renku writing has its dangers, and the most obvious is that a poem will fall apart if the poets fail to unite their efforts. To safeguard against this hazard a number of rules have been laid down. In order to escape from monotony, for example, certain words may not be repeated within the span of two, three, or more verses. The syllable pattern is predetermined: a triplet with the 5-7-5 syllable pattern has to be alternated with a couplet with 7-7, a renku always starting with a triplet and ending with a couplet. Most important, the poem should show a consistent progression in terms of rhythm, imagery, and diction. In a renku of thirty-six verses (the type favored by Bashō in his later years) the first six verses are considered an introductory part, where each verse should be calm in tone, familiar in wording, and moderate in viewpoint, keeping the reader in suspense for more exciting things to come. The next twenty-four verses constitute the main body of the poem; in this part any verse can surprise the reader with its novel style, striking theme or quaint image. The last six verses are the finale; the quick tempo, colorful imagery, and intense language must gradually be muted. Of an infinite number of permissible subjects, cherry blossoms and the moon are traditionally held to be the most interesting, and they had better be woven in at some point. As a very general rule, cherry blossoms should appear in the seventeenth and thirty-fifth verses of a thirty-six-verse renku, while the moon is expected to enter the poem in the fifth, thirteenth, and twenty-ninth verses. These and many other rules of composition are imposed upon each renku poet, making his task not at all an easy one; he has to be an individual and part of the team at the same time. Too original a verse is not commendable since it does not fit well with the rest of the verses, while too conforming a verse makes the poem monotonous.

Bashō was a superb renku writer. He participated in renku writing throughout his career, producing a great number of verses. It can be argued that he poured more energy into renku than into haiku, since the former is a more demanding form. According to someone who was close to him in his last years, Bashō always conceded that in the art of haiku many of his students were his equals, but in the craft of renku writing he believed he alone held the innermost secrets. For the usually modest poet that is a rather unexpected remark, but in view of the evidence it must be said to be true. If we look at renku written in the 1680s and 1690s, we see at once that those composed with Bashō as leader of the team are clearly the best.

Bashō's renku, like his haiku, changed in style as years went by. The pattern of change is virtually the same: he began with a witty, pedantic style and gradually became more serious and somber. Of numerous renku he had a hand in we shall select two and take a close look at them. One is "A Winter Shower" ("Shigure"), which exemplifies his earlier style; the other is "The Summer Moon" ("Natsu no Tsuki"), which can be considered representative of his later works. Each poem consists of thirty-six verses, like most of the renku composed by Bashō and his disciples in his maturity.

I *"A Winter Shower"*

"A Winter Shower" was written early in the winter of 1684. Bashō was then staying in Nagoya, and some local poets, who knew his reputation in Edo, composed several renku under his guidance. In the case of "A Winter Shower," five amateur poets joined Bashō in the making. They were a rice dealer, Tsuboi Tokoku (1656?–90); a lumber merchant, Katō Jūgo (1654–1717); a textile retailer, Okada Yasui (1658-1740); a physician, Yamamoto Kakei (1648–1716); and a man named Koike Shōhei of whom little is known. They were all relatively young and still obscure. Bashō, then about forty, was clearly the leader, and his taste and inclinations pervaded the poem.

Apparently they took turns starting off their joint renku, and in the case of "A Winter Shower" it was Tokoku's turn. He composed this verse in the prescribed 5-7-5 syllable pattern:

Tsutsumi-kanete	A cloud, trying to enwrap
Tsuki toriotosu	The moonbeams, momentarily fails—
Shigure kana	A winter shower.

The first verse of a renku, called the *hokku* ("opening verse"), is self-contained in meaning, and that is part of the reason why it evolved into an independent poem, the haiku. We can take this verse as an independent *hokku* (that is, a haiku) and appreciate it all by itself. It is about a winter shower at night: a large, black, swiftly drifting cloud is overhead, and though it looks thick it evidently has a few rifts, for the shower often stops and pale moonbeams fall through them.

To this Jūgo added the second verse in two seven-syllable lines:

Kōri fumiyuku	Someone walks on icy patches,
Mizu no inazuma	Making lightning in the water.

The second verse, called *wakiku,* cannot be independent; it has to complement the first verse and make a single five-line poem when they are put together. Jūgo's verse certainly does so:

Tsutsumi-kanete	A cloud, trying to enwrap
Tsuki toriotosu	The moonbeams, momentarily fails—
Shigure kana	A winter shower.
Kōri fumiyuku	Someone walks on icy patches,
Mizu no inazuma	Making lightning in the water.

Jūgo has now placed a man in the scene. The shower has made

puddles covered with thin ice on the road, and as a passerby steps on them the ice breaks and the water splashes out, looking like small flashes of lightning in the reflected moonlight. To Tokoku's verse, Jūgo's lines have added a focal point and a sense of movement.

Now it was Yasui's turn. He composed the following verse:

Shida no ha o	The New Year's hunter,
Hatsukaribito no	On his back a quiver
Ya ni oite	Adorned with ferns.

We add this to Jūgo's verse and get a new poem:

Kōri fumiyuku	Someone walks on icy patches,
Mizu no inazuma	Making lightning in the water.
Shida no ha o	The New Year's hunter,
Hatsukaribito no	On his back a quiver
Ya ni oite	Adorned with ferns.

Jūgo's couplet now assumes a somewhat different meaning. The season is not winter but early spring, the hour is not night but early morning, and "someone" is not an ordinary passerby but a man going hunting in the New Year's season. Combined, the two verses present a picture of a neatly dressed hunter hurrying to the woods in the chilly morning air. Though it is springtime on the calendar there are still some ice patches on the road, and as he steps on them the water splashes in the early morning sun. The sparkling water is in beautiful contrast to the green ferns, a New Year decoration that adorns the hunter's quiver.

All verses of a renku, except the first and the last, must work two ways like this one of Jūgo's. Each must be a perfect complement to both the preceding and the succeeding verse, in both cases creating an autonomous five-line poem. From the individual poet's point of view, each verse has a double meaning, one conscious and the other unconscious. One of the factors that make renku writing exciting lies in the development of this unconscious meaning. A poet composes a verse, and a few minutes later he finds to his amusement that one of his teammates interprets it in a way he had not thought of. We shall see how this is done in the rest of "A Winter Shower."

The next poet to contribute a verse was Bashō himself. As required, he made up a couplet and added it to Yasui's triplet:

Shida no ha o	The New Year's hunter,
Hatsukaribito no	On his back a quiver
Ya ni oite	Adorned with ferns.
Kita no gomon o	The northern gate is open
Oshiake no haru	And the beginning of springtime.

"The northern gate" is the service entrance of a palace—the main gate is usually in the south. According to Bashō's interpretation, "the New Year's hunter" is not a real hunter hurrying to the woods but a nobleman in a hunter's costume performing a rite of spring in the New Year's season. The harsh, masculine atmosphere has become more elegant and courtly. In passing we might note that in Japanese "open" and "begin" are one word, a choice reminiscent of the word play Bashō employed in his early haiku.

The elegant mood is continued with a shocking twist in the next verse by Kakei:

Kita no gomon o	The northern gate is open
Oshiake no haru	And the beginning of springtime.
Maguso kaku	Over a fan
Ōgi ni kaze no	That brushes away the horse dung,
Uchikasumi	A hazy breeze.

The hunting theme has disappeared. Now that winter is over, a nobleman is going out for a stroll, attended by several pages. As they step through the service gate they encounter some horse dung, upon which one of the pages takes out his fan and sweeps the dry, light dung out of the way. Even using such crude material, the verse is hardly vulgar; it presents a lovely spring scene with a graceful courtier and his pages in front of a palace.

The setting moves from the palace grounds to the countryside when Shōhei adds his verse to Kakei's:

Maguso kaku	Over a fan

Ōgi ni kaze no	That brushes away the horse dung,
Uchikasumi	A hazy breeze.
Chanoyuja oshimu	The tea master loves
Nobe no tanpopo	Dandelion flowers on the roadside.

Here a tea master on his country stroll, finding that horse dung has buried some dandelions, takes pity and removes it with his fan. We might remember that in the Japanese tea ceremony plain, commonplace beauty like that of a dandelion is especially admired. Shōhei's addition shifts the mood from courtly grace to rusticity.

The next verse, contributed by Jūgo, focuses on the tea master's life:

Chanoyuja oshimu	The tea master loves
Nobe no tanpopo	Dandelion flowers on the roadside.
Rōtage ni	At home the young maiden
Mono yomu musume	Reads an ancient romance
Kashizukite	In a lovely pose.

This is a quiet, peaceful life indeed. While the father goes out to admire wild dandelions, the daughter stays home and reads an old romance. Being a tea master's daughter, she must be lovely, graceful, and well versed in classical Japanese literature.

The scene becomes more dramatic with Tokoku's couplet:

Rōtage ni	At home the young maiden
Mono yomu musume	Reads an ancient romance
Kashizukite	In a lovely pose.
Tōro futatsu ni	Two decorated lanterns
Nasake kuraburu	Competing to reveal the depth of love.

The girl is in a dilemma, just like the heroine of the romance she is reading. She is being wooed by two young men, each of whom has sent her a beautiful lantern. The lanterns are by her side and unconsciously disturb her as she reads.

The theme of rivalry is expanded by Bashō, who composed the next verse:

Tōro futatsu ni	Two decorated lanterns
Nasake kuraburu	Competing to reveal the depth of love.
Tsuyu hagi no	Dewdrops and bush clover
Sumō chikara o	Wrestling with each other
Erabarezu	In a perfect match.

In the garden outside, bush clover is in bloom. Over the numerous small pink blossoms blooming on long slender stems, shining dewdrops are sprinkled. The dew tries to weigh down the flower, and the flexible stems attempt to resist its weight: this is a perfect match. The rivalry between shining dewdrops and pink bush clover can be compared to the rivalry in love represented by two decorated lanterns.

The pretty scene in an autumn garden is transferred to an entirely different setting by Yasui:

Tsuyu hagi no	Dewdrops and bush clover
Sumō chikara o	Wrestling with each other
Erabarezu	In a perfect match.
Soba sae aoshi	Even buckwheat noodles are green
Shigaraki no bō	At an inn in Shigaraki.

Shigaraki, an old town near Lake Biwa that flourished during the prime of Buddhism in Japan, is known for its high-quality green tea. Now a traveler who has stopped at an inn in Shigaraki is served buckwheat noodles together with the famous tea. The noodles, made from the year's earliest crops, look somewhat green. To the traveler's eyes, their green blends perfectly with the color of the tea. And that bond has something in common with the perfectly matched dewdrops and bush clover he sees in the garden adjoining his room.

This traveler is given a more specific identity in the next verse by Tokoku:

Soba sae aoshi	Even buckwheat noodles are green
Shigaraki no bō	At an inn in Shigaraki.
Asazukuyo	The moon at dawn–
Sugorokuuchi no	A backgammon player begins
Tabine shite	Another day of traveling.

There is a subtle harmony between the green noodles and the twilight moon. There is also a relationship between the old town of Shigaraki and Japanese backgammon, an ancient court game; we can imagine a group of noblemen enjoying a game of backgammon at a flourishing palace in Shigaraki centuries ago. The humor of the verse lies in the fact that backgammon had since lost its social status; it was now a gambler's game. This particular gambler who came to Shigaraki drank too much of the famous tea last night and did not sleep well. Usually a late riser, he has risen unusually early this morning and is taking his leave, in his sleepy head cursing the green tea and, along with it, the noodles that had the same greenish color.

Kakei had another explanation as to why the gambler woke so early:

Asazukuyo	The moon at dawn–
Sugorokuuchi no	A backgammon player begins
Tabine shite	Another day of traveling.
Beni kau michi ni	On the way to buy safflower,
Hototogisu kiku	A cuckoo's call.

The backgammon player is a safflower dealer by profession. Safflower, in order to be made into good dyes, has to be plucked early in the morning. So the man leaves the inn at dawn and is now walking along a country lane. On both sides of the lane are safflower farms, and the orange-colored flowers are beautiful in the morning half-light. Suddenly, from nowhere, a cuckoo is heard.

Now Yasui, adding a triplet, changes the mood. The image of a gambler fades out, and that of an elegant young lady emerges. It is in this way that the renku is said to have anticipated the modern film technique of montage.

Beni kau michi ni	On the way to buy safflower,
Hototogisu kiku	A cuckoo's call.
Shinobu ma no	To kill the leisurely hours
Waza tote hina o	At the hiding place,
Tsukuriiru	She makes a doll.

The lady is hiding away in a small country house. We are not told why she has to hide, but we suppose there is some romantic reason, since she is apparently young and well born. Having plenty of time to kill, she entertains herself by making pretty dolls. She is now walking along a country lane to buy some safflower needed for her doll-making, when she hears a cuckoo in the distance.

Making a doll is an elegant pastime. This woman also admires a cuckoo's song. She must be a noble, well-educated lady, perhaps from the Empress's court or some such place. Hence Jūgo's addition:

Shinobu ma no	To kill the leisurely hours
Waza tote hina o	At the hiding place,
Tsukuriiru	She makes a doll.
Myōbu no kimi yori	From a lady at the Empress's court
Kome nando kosu	Rice and other gifts have come.

A certain lady at the Empress's court is a good friend of this woman and writes letters to help fill her idle hours at the hideaway. This time she sent gifts.

The elegant picture with two court ladies in its center disappears when a verse by Kakei is added:

Myōbu no kimi yori	From a lady at the Empress's court
Kome nando kosu	Rice and other gifts have come.
Magaki made	A brushwood fence lies
Tsunami no mizu ni	In ruins, after the far-reaching
Kuzureyuki	Tidal waves' attack.

This is a village devastated by tidal waves. Some villagers who survived the disaster have come back and begun to salvage what remains. The imperial family, taking pity on the survivors, immediately had a lady-in-waiting send rice and other gifts to the disaster area.

The story then takes a whimsical direction. The renku is nearing its midpoint, and something is needed to excite the participants. The poet who took on this responsibility was none other than Bashō:

Magaki made	A brushwood fence lies
Tsunami no mizu ni	In ruins, after the far-reaching
Kuzureyuki	Tidal waves' attack.
Hotoke kūtaru	The fish, when slit open,
Uo hodokikeri	Reveals a Buddha it has eaten.

Tidal waves often leave a number of fish stranded on land. On this occasion one of these fish, a huge one, discloses an image of Buddha when it is slit open. This is a miracle, the kind of incident often told of in folklore.

The scene of devastation is quickly transformed when Jūgo adds his three lines:

Hotoke kūtaru	The fish, when slit open,
Uo hodokikeri	Reveals a Buddha it has eaten.
Agata furu	Of an old illustrious clan,
Hanami Jirō to	The man is called Hanami Jirō
Aogarete	And commands high respect in the district.

Hanami Jirō is a fictional name, but it carries a definite connotation. Hanami means "blossom viewing." Jirō, a masculine given name, indicates that he is the second son. The stereotyped image of a second son in Japan is that of a sociable, carefree, large-hearted man. Furthermore, in this particular case the man is from an old, illustrious family. Probably he is now giving a blossom-viewing party for hundreds of people in the village; he is the sort who enjoys entertaining. His chef, busy preparing the banquet, slits open a large fish and finds an image of Buddha in its stomach. All the guests witness the miracle and respect Hanami Jirō all the more for it.

The image of a wealthy, charitable man is further cultivated by Tokoku:

Agata furu	Of an old illustrious clan,
Hanami Jirō to	The man is called Hanami Jirō
Aogarete	And commands high respect in the district.
Genge sumire no	Six *tan* of farmland
Hatake rokutan	Covered with violets and red clover.

Six *tan* are about fifteen acres, not at all a negligible amount of land in Japan; many Japanese farmers owned less. To Hanami Jirō, however, six *tan* are nothing; he simply leaves the land to wild violets and red clover and enjoys the flowers when they bloom. We might visualize this flower-covered farm in front of his imposing mansion; we then have a quiet, peaceful country scene in sharp contrast to the drama of the preceding verses.

The next poet, Bashō, also liked the restoration of the peaceful scene. So he continued on a similar mood:

Genge sumire no	Six *tan* of farmland
Hatake rokutan	Covered with violets and red clover.
Ureshige ni	Joyously
Saezuru hibari	The skylark sings:
Chiri chiri to	*Chiri chiri* . . .

Bashō's addition provides a focal point for the spreading farmland scene, a tiny bird in the vast expanse. It also adds a feeling of movement and an aural image. *Chiri chiri*, Bashō's own onomatopoeia, is suggestive of the skylark's clear, serene chirp.

Yasui contributed a further variation to the springtime scene:

Ureshige ni	Joyously
Saezuru hibari	The skylark sings:
Chiri chiri to	*Chiri chiri* . . .
Mahiru no uma no	At noonday, how drowsy
Nebutagao nari	Is the horse's face!

It is noon on a spring day. The sun is warm, the breeze is pleasant, and even a horse becomes sleepy. The contrast between the tiny skylark and the lumbering horse, between the former's clear singing and the latter's long, rather dumb face, is quite effective.

What is the horse doing, and where is the setting? Tokoku gives specific details:

Mahiru no uma no	At noonday, how drowsy
Nebutagao nari	Is the horse's face!
Okazaki ya	Here at Okazaki,

Yahagi no hashi no	Yahagi Bridge extends
Nagaki kana	Endlessly onwards.

Okazaki, a town near Nagoya, was famous for its Yahagi Bridge, then one of the longest bridges in Japan. Now at noon on a warm spring day, a horse with a traveler on its back is crossing the bridge. The other side seems to come no closer, and the traveler, hearing only the monotonous repetition of the horse's ambling footsteps, becomes drowsy himself.

The focus of the poem is moving from the horse to the man on its back. Kakei makes this definite:

Okazaki ya	Here at Okazaki,
Yahagi no hashi no	Yahagi Bridge extends
Nagaki kana	Endlessly onwards.
Shōya no matsu o	Noticing the headman's pine,
Yomite okurinu	He writes a poem and sends it off.

Yahagi Bridge is famous in classical Japanese literature. The traveler is excited to be crossing the bridge and feels like writing a poem. He looks around and finds a fitting subject: an old pine tree at the town headman's house. Whereupon he writes a poem and sends it to a friend in his village who shares his interest in poetry.

After a few relatively descriptive verses, the renku is becoming more like a story again. Yasui enhances it by introducing a dramatic incident:

Shōya no matsu o	Noticing the headman's pine,
Yomite okurinu	He writes a poem and sends it off.
Suteshi ko wa	That abadoned child:
Shiba karu take ni	Has he grown old enough
Nobitsuran	To work in the woods?

The traveler once had a sorrowful experience. When he was young, certain unfortunate circumstances required him to abandon his beloved son in infancy. After long hours of agonized thinking, he decided to leave the baby under the pine tree of his village chief, who he knew was a kind, considerate man. Now looking at a pine tree at the local headman's house, he recalls the experience and sends a poem to the foster parents inquiring about the son he deserted.

The man who abandoned the child is a samurai who resigned from service and who has been unemployed ever since. Thus Jūgo develops the plot:

Suteshi ko wa	That abandoned child:
Shiba karu take ni	Has he grown old enough
Nobitsuran	To work in the woods?
Misoka o samuku	The last day of the year, it is cold
Katana uru toshi	And the sword has been sold.

An agelong Japanese custom prescribed that all debts be paid off by the last day of the year. This warrior, unemployed for many years, cannot raise enough money and is forced to sell his status symbol, the sword. The day is cold, not only because it is winter but because his hut is so shabby. Sitting alone in a scantly furnished room, the samurai thinks of the child he deserted because of poverty.

The renku's mood is a melancholy one at this point. Kakei, by interpreting Jūgo's couplet differently and adding his own triplet, completely dispels the gloom:

Misoka o samuku	The last day of the year, it is cold
Katana uru toshi	And the sword has been sold.
Yuki no kyō	Here comes a lover
Go no kuni no kasa	Of the snow, wearing a rare
Mezurashiki	Wu-style hat.

The samurai who has sold the sword does not mind poverty at all; he is rather enjoying it in the way many Chinese recluses did. Now he is delighted by the visit of his friend, who has a similar poetic taste. Long in the avant-garde, the friend always wears tasteful but unconventional things. Today he is sporting a rare hat made in the style of Wu, a state where people's costumes were distinctly different from those of other Chinese kingdoms. On his exotic hat lies a thin layer of the snow that has begun to fall outside. Probably the two friends will have an informal party, enjoying the view of the snow and composing poems about it.

A new element enters this quiet scene when Bashō decides to take the "lover" to be an amorous man:

Yuki no kyō	Here comes a lover
Go no kuni no kasa	Of the snow, wearing a rare
Mezurashiki	Wu-style hat.
Eri ni Takao ga	For his muffler, Miss Takao
Katasode o toku	Tears off a sleeve of her kimono.

The man with the Wu-style hat is a fashionable town dandy. On a snowy day he comes to Yoshiwara, the gay quarters of Edo, and holds a snow-viewing party. Many lovely courtesans are present, but the one who waits on him with special intimacy is a remarkably beautiful woman called Miss Takao, a nickname deriving from a famous geisha of the early seventeenth century. As the party becomes wilder, Miss Takao tears off her sleeve and gives it to him for a muffler, whispering to him that it will make him feel her warmth even on the coldest day.

The increasing sensuality is brought to a peak by Jūgo:

Eri ni Takao ga	For his muffler, Miss Takao
Katasode o toku	Tears off a sleeve of her kimono.
Adabito to	With this dearest one
Taru o hitsugi ni	He could drink up the whole barrel
Nomihosan	And make it a coffin!

A Don Juan lives for love and dies for love. With a rare beauty like Miss Takao attending him, he could blissfully drink himself to death.

In a fine display of wit, Tokoku replaces the amorous man with a Buddhist monk:

Adabito to	With this dearest one
Taru o hitsugi ni	He could drink up the whole barrel
Nomihosan	And make it a coffin!
Keshi no hitoe ni	A Zen monk, his name known
Na o kobosu zen	With the falling petals of a poppy.

A poppy is gorgeous, but it falls in three or four days and becomes an uncouth skeleton. A truly enlightened Zen monk, knowing the brevity of human existence, might live a "gorgeous" life, totally different from the asceticism usually associated with a Buddhist monk. This particular Zen monk does just that; he is waited on by a beautiful courtesan and drinks quantities of rice wine. His name, however, is widely respected as that of a monk of the highest order in Zen.

Then as Bashō takes over, the gaiety recedes and in its place emerges a somber atmosphere that was to become typical of his later haiku:

Keshi no hitoe ni	A Zen monk, his name known
Na o kobosu zen	With the falling petals of a poppy.
Mikazuki no	The crescent moon—
Higashi wa kuraku	The eastern sky is dark,
Kane no koe	And the sound of a bell.

This can be taken as an evening scene at a Zen monastery lying amid tall trees deep in the woods. Breaking the tranquillity, a temple bell tolls the hour of the evening. Looking toward the west, the monk sees the crescent moon in the sky which is still slightly ruddy. Hearing the temple bell and gazing at the western sky, he once again comes to realize the transitoriness of all things that live, the same recognition he had arrived at earlier on seeing a poppy flower fall.

The symbolic meaning of Bashō's verse fades out, and only the visually beautiful scene remains when Yasui adds his couplet:

Mikazuki no	The crescent moon—
Higashi wa kuraku	The eastern sky is dark,
Kane no koe	And the sound of a bell.
Shūko kasukani	On the autumn lake, faintly
Koto kaesu mono	Someone playing an old tune on the koto.

In the dusk a lake extends into the distance. As the temple bell falls silent, there are heard the soft, delicate sounds of a koto, a stringed instrument that sounds somewhat like a harp. They are the notes of an old melody; no doubt the musician is remembering bygone days.

The next poet, Tokoku, interprets Yasui's couplet differently. The koto player is not a lady at a lakeside hideaway recalling her youth but a recluse enjoying himself aboard a boat:

Shūko kasukani	On the autumn lake, faintly
Koto kaesu mono	Someone playing an old tune on the koto.
Niru koto o	Instead of taking them home
Yurushite haze o	To cook, he lets go
Hanachikeru	The cobies he has caught.

The recluse has both a koto and a fishing rod in the boat. Floating on the calm water under the clear blue sky he now plays some familiar melodies on the koto, now enjoys coby fishing. Of course he never takes home the cobies he catches; if he did so the pleasure of fishing would be spoiled.

Kakei's interpretation of Tokoku's lines results in a rather comic scene, a refreshing change of mood:

Niru koto o	Instead of taking them home
Yurushite haze o	To cook, he lets go
Hanachikeru	The cobies he has caught.
Koe yoki nebutsu	A serene voice praying to Buddha
Yabu o hedatsuru	Is heard through the bush.

According to Kakei's interpretation, the man doing the fishing is not a happy recluse but an ordinary man who *does* want to take his cobies home. While fishing on the shore, he hears a Buddisht monk chanting a prayer at a small hut behind a bush. Reminded of Buddha's admonition not to kill living creatures, he begins to feel uneasy about his plan to take cobies home and eat them.

Yasui then introduces his own hero, another interesting contrast to the praying monk:

Koe yoki nebutsu	A serene voice praying to Buddha
Yabu o hedatsuru	Is heard through the bush.

Kage usuki	The oil lamp is feebly burning,
Andon keshi ni	Yet the man cannot stir himself up
Okiwabite	To go and put out the light.

The man, probably aged and retired, lives next to the monk's hut. After supper he usually takes a brief nap, but tonight he has slept for quite a long time. Waking up, he finds it is past midnight; he really should put out the light and go back to sleep. But after that long nap he feels hazy in the head and even more tired than before; he just cannot work up enough energy to get up and walk to the lamp, which is only a few steps away. His laziness is in sharp contrast to the diligence of his neighbor, who no doubt will continue to recite sutras all through the night.

The sleepy old man changes into a young lover and the poem acquires a sensual cast again when Jūgo takes over:

Kage usuki	The oil lamp is feebly burning,
Andon keshi ni	Yet the man cannot stir himself up
Okiwabite	To go and put out the light.
Omoikanetsu mo	Not knowing what to do,
Yoru no obi hiku	He pulls the sash of her nightwear.

The young man has just sneaked into his sweetheart's room at night. She is asleep, with a feeble light on. He would like to put out the light, but that might attract the attention of someone still awake in the household. Not knowing what to do, he lightly pulls the girl's sash to wake her up.

The love motif is carried on by Kakei, who has had the difficult task of introducing blossoms into the poem, for his verse is the thirty-fifth, where cherry blossoms should appear:

Omoikanetsu mo	Not knowing what to do,
Yoru no obi hiku	He pulls the sash of her nightwear.
Kogare tobu	The lovelorn soul
Tamashii hana no	Flying into the shade of the blossoms
Kage ni iru	It has been pining for.

It has been a common idea in Japanese romance that a lovelorn soul leaves its body and goes to meet the sweetheart when two lovers are forced to live apart. The "blossoms" here of course represent the lovely woman for whom this young man has been pining. He loves her with such intensity that his soul would leave his body if he were to be separated from her.

Bashō, now concluding the entire poem, reinterprets Kakei's lines. In his interpretation the cherry blossoms are real, and the lover is a poet who admires them with a passion so intense that at his death his soul can find a resting place only in their shade. Thus the last lines of the renku are highly romantic:

Kogare tobu	The lovelorn soul
Tamashii hana no	Flying into the shade of the blossoms
Kage ni iru	It has been pining for.
Sono mochi no hi o	I wish I could do the same
Ware mo onajiku	On that day of the full moon.

The lines allude to a famous tanka by Priest Saigyō (1118–90) who, like Bashō, forsook his samurai status to live closer to the heart of nature. The poem, written toward the end of his life, eloquently expresses his love of cherry blossoms:

Negawakuwa	Could I but die
Hana no moto nite	Under the cherry blossoms
Haru shinan	In springtime
Sono kisaragi no	On the night of the full moon
Mochizuki no koro	In the second month of the year.

Saigyō's wish was fulfilled; he is said to have passed away on the night of the full moon in the second month of the year, when cherry blossoms were at their best. Bashō, always an ardent admirer of Saigyō, visualizes that medieval poet's soul flying into the shade of cherry blossoms and wishes he could do the same.

We now have "A Winter Shower" in its entirety. Its thirty-six verses, all put together, read as follows:

Shigure	A Winter shower
Tsutsumi-kanete	A cloud, trying to enwrap
Tsuki toriotosu	The moonbeams, momentarily fails—
Shigure kana	A winter shower.

The Renku

Kōri fumiyuku *Mizu no inazuma*	Someone walks on icy patches, Making lightning in the water.
Shida no ha o *Hatsukaribito no* *Ya ni oite*	The New Year's hunter, On his back a quiver Adorned with ferns.
Kita no gomon o *Oshiake no haru*	The northern gate is open And the beginning of springtime.
Maguso kaku *Ōgi ni kaze no* *Uchikasumi*	Over a fan That brushes away the horse dung, A hazy breeze.
Chanoyuja oshimu *Nobe no tanpopo*	The tea master loves Dandelion flowers on the roadside.
Rōtage ni *Mono yomu musume* *Kashizukite*	At home the young maiden Reads an ancient romance In a lovely pose.
Tōro futatsu ni *Nasake kuraburu*	Two decorated lanterns Competing to reveal the depth of love.
Tsuyu hagi no *Sumō chikara o* *Erabarezu*	Dewdrops and bush clover Wrestling with each other In a perfect match.
Soba sae aoshi *Shigaraki no bō*	Even buckwheat noodles are green At an inn in Shigaraki.
Asazukuyo *Sugorokuuchi no* *Tabine shite*	The moon at dawn– A backgammon player begins Another day of traveling.
Beni kau michi ni *Hototogisu kiku*	On the way to buy safflower, A cuckoo's call.

Shinobu ma no
Waza tote hina o
Tsukuriiru

To kill the leisurely hours
At the hiding place,
She makes a doll.

Myōbu no kimi yori
Kome nando kosu

From a lady at the Empress's court
Rice and other gifts have come.

Magaki made
Tsunami no mizu ni
Kuzureyuku

A brushwood fence lies
In ruins, after the far-reaching
Tidal wave's attack.

Hotoke kūtaru
Uo hodokikeri

The fish, when slit open,
Reveals a Buddha it has eaten.

Agata furu
Hanami Jirō to
Aogarete

Of an old illustrious clan
The man is called Hanami Jirō
And commands high respect in the district.

Genge sumire no
Hatake rokutan

Six *tan* of farmland
Covered with violets and red clover.

Ureshige ni
Saezuru hibari
Chiri chiri to

Joyously
The skylark sings:
Chiri chiri . . .

Mahiru no uma no
Nebutagao nari

At noonday, how drowsy
Is the horse's face!

Okazaki ya
Yahagi no hashi no
Nagaki kana

Here at Okazaki,
Yahagi Bridge extends
Endlessly onwards.

Shōya no matsu o
Yomite okurinu

Noticing the headman's pine,
He writes a poem and sends it off.

Suteshi ko wa
Shiba karu take ni
Nobitsuran

That abandoned child:
Has he grown old enough
To work in the woods?

Misoka o samuku *Katana uru toshi*	The last day of the year, it is cold And the sword has been sold.
Yuki no kyō *Go no kuni no kasa* *Mezurashiki*	Here comes a lover Of the snow, wearing a rare Wu-style hat.
Eri ni Takao ga *Katasode o toku*	For his muffler, Miss Takao Tears off a sleeve of her kimono.
Adabito to *Taru o hitsugi ni* *Nomihosan*	With this dearest one He could drink up the whole barrel And make it a coffin!
Keshi no hitoe ni *Na o kobosu zen*	A Zen monk, his name known With the falling petals of a poppy.
Mikazuki no *Higashi wa kuraku* *Kane no koe*	The crescent moon— The eastern sky is dark, And the sound of a bell.
Shūko kasukani *Koto kaesu mono*	On the autumn lake, faintly Someone playing an old tune on the koto.
Niru koto o *Yurushite haze o* *Hanachikeru*	Instead of taking them home To cook, he lets go The cobies he has caught.
Koe yoki nebutsu *Yabu o hedatsuru*	A serene voice praying to Buddha Is heard through the bush.
Kage usuki *Andon keshi ni* *Okiwabite*	The oil lamp is feebly burning, Yet the man cannot stir himself up To go and put out the light.
Omoikanetsu mo *Yoru no obi hiku*	Not knowing what to do, He pulls the sash of her nightwear.

Kogare tobu	The lovelorn soul
Tamashii hana no	Flying into the shade of the blossoms
Kage ni iru	It has been pining for.
Sono mochi no hi o	I wish I could do the same
Ware mo onajiku	On that day of the full moon.

On the whole, "A Winter Shower" can be said to be a poem of youthful imagination. It is romantic in the sense that it tries to encompass the whole range of nature's beauty and man's passion, exploring areas of life outside the experience of the average person. Its scope ranges from the felicitous picture of a skylark cheerfully twittering across a spacious field covered with wild flowers to the devastation of a village destroyed by tidal waves. The aspects of human life and emotion it reflects extend from the attitude of an epicurean who carouses through the night with courtesans to that of a stoic who recites sutras till dawn at a humble lakeside cottage. There are suggestions of human drama rather unusual in traditional Japanese poetry, among them the samurai forced to desert his infant child and the young men competing for a maiden's hand. There are supernatural elements, too, such as the fish containing a Buddha and the lovelorn soul flying into the shade of cherry blossoms. Different types of beauty and a wide variety of sentiments mingle and flow through the poem.

"A Winter Shower" has always been admired. Together with four other renku composed at the same time by this group of poets, it was included in *The Winter Sun,* and has been considered one of the outstanding classics of the genre. Many readers have since been moved to publish their thoughts about the poem, though they differed considerably in the interpretation of individual verses. That is what is expected of a good renku: it is intended to stimulate the reader's imagination, asking him to join the verse-writing party. In a renku, even the author does not have an exclusive claim to the meaning of the verse he writes.

II *"The Summer Moon"*

"The Summer Moon" is one of the finest renku to spring from

Bashō's later literary activities. It was written in the summer of 1690, when Bashō was enjoying a leisurely sojourn in the Kyoto area after the long journey to the far north. Two of his leading disciples, Kyorai and Bonchō, joined him in composing this renku of thirty-six verses. Kyorai, born in a samurai family in Kyushu, had given up serving as such and was then living a carefree life in Kyoto. Bonchō, a physician by profession, had only recently become Bashō's student, but he had quickly distinguished himself for his poetic talent. Bashō was about forty-six.

In composing "The Summer Moon" the three poets took regular turns in contributing verses, although, as usual, Bashō was the team leader and must have given many words of advice to his teammates. The opening verse was by Bonchō:

Ichinaka wa	Above a town
Mono no nioi ya	Filled with the odors of things,
Natsu no tsuki	The summer moon.

The hokku impressionistically presents a vignette of lively town life on a hot summer evening. The streets are crowded, and the air is filled with smells of all kinds of things—cooked fish, boiled vegetables, sweat, horse dung—so that the evening seems even hotter. Above all this hustle and bustle a cool white moon floats in the sky.

The opening verse has a large-scale setting that extends both horizontally and vertically. The next verse, composed by Bashō, focuses on the ground:

Ichinaka wa	Above a town
Mono no nioi ya	Filled with the odors of things,
Natsu no tsuki	The summer moon.
Atsushi atsushi to	"It's hot!" "It's hot!"
Kado kado no koe	Murmurs are heard in the frontyards.

The reader now comes closer to the human scene. The evening is so warm and humid that people cannot stay indoors; they sit outside to cool off. Looking up, they see the distant, beautiful moon.

When Kyorai adds his verse to Bashō's, the summer night in

town recedes, and in its place there emerges a farming village:

Atsushi atsushi to	"It's hot!" "It's hot!"
Kado kado no koe	Murmurs are heard in the frontyards.
Nibangusa	Though the second weeding
Tori mo hatasazu	Is not yet over, rice plants
Ho ni idete	Shoot out their ears.

Rice plants usually begin to grow ears about the time farmers finish the third weeding. This year it has been so hot that rice plants are growing unusually fast and shooting out ears several weeks early. The farmers, though they complain about the heat, are pleased about their rice plants. Here is a pleasant change of mood from the malodorous town to the fresh air of the country, from the townsfolk's grumbles to the farmers' murmurs that conceal joy.

The camera now takes a closeup, as it were, of the countryfolk. That is what Bonchō's lines do:

Nibangusa	Though the second weeding
Tori mo hatasazu	Is not yet over, rice plants
Ho ni idete	Shoot out their ears.
Hai uchitataku	Ashes are brushed off a dried sardine
Urume ichimai	Just taken from the fire.

The farmers are eating lunch. They are very busy, for it is weeding time; unable to take a long lunch break, they eat dried sardines, which are easy to prepare. One of the farmers has now taken a sardine from the fire and is brushing off the ashes. The busy life on a farm is crystallized in this act.

Now it is Bashō's turn. As he adds his lines, we find ourselves in a small teashop in a remote district:

Hai uchitataku	Ashes are brushed off a dried sardine
Urume ichimai	Just taken from the fire.
Kono suji wa	Those who live in this area
Gin mo mishirazu	Have never seen a silver coin.
Fujiyusa yo	What a wretched place!

This is indeed an uncivilized area; the proprietress at the teashop, broiling a dried sardine for a traveler's lunch, does not use a net on the fire and burns the fish. To pay for his lunch the traveler gives a silver coin to the proprietress, who refuses it because she does not know what it is. Flabbergasted, he groans to himself: "What a wretched place!"

Who could this traveler be? His identity is elucidated when Kyorai contributes his lines:

Kono suji wa	Those who live in this area
Gin mo mishirazu	Have never seen a silver coin.
Fujiyusa yo	What a wretched place!
Tada tohyōshi ni	The fellow wears at his waist
Nagaki wakizashi	An absurdly long sword.

The traveler represents a peculiar type of townsman who often appears in seventeenth-century Japanese literature. He is a young dandy, handsome and well dressed, who is too conceited to earn his living by working industriously. He wears an excessively long sword to show off his identity and drifts from one place to another seeking a gambling house. Now, at this remote little inn, he sneers at the country folk who do not even recognize a silver coin, commonplace to a gambler.

The image of a handsome gambler soon fades out. Replacing him in Bonchō's triplet is a little man who carries an absurdly long sword to cover up his inferiority complex. The poem is becoming increasingly comic:

Tada tohyōshi ni	The fellow wears at his waist
Nagaki wakizashi	An absurdly long sword.
Kusamura ni	From the cluster of grass
Kawazu kowagaru	A frightening creature—a frog
Yūmagure	In the evening dusk.

That long sword is not enough to overcome the man's timidity. Walking alone on a lonely road in the evening dusk, he starts in fear when he sees something moving in a clump of grass at the roadside. Before his frightened eyes there hops out a little creature—nothing but an ordinary frog.

The last few verses have been rather rustic and crude. It is now high time for a more elegant atmosphere. Bashō, the next poet in line, skillfully produces the modulation:

Kusamura ni	From the cluster of grass
Kawazu kowagaru	A frightening creature—a frog
Yūmagure	In the evening dusk.
Fuki no me tori ni	The lady hunting for butterburs
Ando yuri kesu	Jerks her lantern, and the light is gone.

Late in the evening a noblewoman is in her garden picking some edible young butterbur shoots, when suddenly she notices a stir in a clump of grass nearby. With a little scream she steps back; the lantern she holds is shaken so hard the light goes out. Without a word to describe the lady, the lines suggest her lovely figure against the rustic background.

The poem keeps a forward progression. The graceful lady turns into a nun when Kyorai reinterprets Bashō's lines:

Fuki no me tori ni	The lady hunting for butterburs
Ando yuri kesu	Jerks her lantern, and the light is gone.
Dōshin no	She set her mind
Okori wa hana no	On Nirvana, when cherry blossoms
Tsubomu toki	Were still in bud.

The scene is probably a small, secluded hut in the country. The nun is picking butterburs in her backyard, when a sudden gust blows out the light in her lantern; her attempt to guard the lantern against the wind by a quick motion of her hand is too late. The way the light has gone out is just like a human life being terminated by a great cosmic power. The nun is led to recall her young days when, suddenly realizing the fragility of life, she decided to become a nun.

Butterburs and cherry blossoms have produced a colorful picture. Bonchō erases it all, introducing a harsh wintry mood:

Dōshin no	She set her mind
Okori wa hana no	On Nirvana, when cherry blossoms
Tsubomu toki	Were still in bud.

Noto no Nanao no	At Nanao in Noto Province
Fuyu wa sumi uki	It's hard to live through a wintertime.

Nanao is a small fishing village on the northern coast of Japan, known for its severe winter cold. Here an aged woman who renounced the world in her youth is performing an ascetic exercise in the midst of winter.

Bashō accentuates the barren winter atmosphere by bringing in a senile man:

Noto no Nanao no	At Nanao in Noto Province
Fuku wa sumi uki	It's hard to live through a wintertime.
Uo no hone	A man, infirm
Shiwaburu made no	With age, slowly sucks
Oi o mite	A fish bone.

The Buddhist overtone is gone. A toothless old fisherman, who used to be proud of his strong teeth, slowly sucks a fish bone. This is the wintertime of human life.

Then, as Kyorai takes over, the poor fishing village on the northern coast suddenly becomes a noblewoman's mansion in a suburb of the capital:

Uo no hone	A man, infirm
Shiwaburu made no	With age, slowly sucks
Oi o mite	A fish bone.
Machibito ireshi	He lets a lover in,
Komikado no kagi	Unlocking the small gate.

Late at night the lady's young lover secretly comes for a visit and knocks at the small side gate. The old gatekeeper, putting down the fish bone he has been sucking, totters out to let him in. The gatekeeper's senility suggests that his mistress is of an ancient family but is now out of favor with the court. The lover, in contrast, is a high-ranking prince who likes amorous adventures.

In another quick change of mood, Bonchō replaces the ancient court romance with a rather humorous scene from a contemporary commoner's life:

Machibito ireshi	He lets a lover in,
Komikado no kagi	Unlocking the small gate.
Tachi kakari	The maidservants
Byōbu o tausu	Trying to take a peep
Onago domo	Knocks down the screen!

The setting is probably a rich merchant's house. During his absence his beautiful daughter's lover bribes the gatekeeper and sneaks in through the side gate. But he cannot escape the attention of the maidservants, who always have a quick eye for this sort of thing. They cluster behind a standing screen, trying to catch a glimpse of their mistress's sweetheart. But their excessive curiosity betrays them: they press against the screen so hard that, to their horror, it falls down and exposes them.

The amorous gaiety is somewhat subdued by Bashō, who interprets Bonchō's lines differently:

Tachi kakari	The maidservants
Byōbu o tausu	Trying to take a peep
Onago domo	Knocks down the screen!
Yudono wa take no	On the bathroom floor,
Sunoko wabishiki	A modest bamboo mat.

The scene is a country inn far from commercial centers. A handsome young man, with refined manners, has registered here this evening. All the maids are curious, and when the guest takes a bath in the modest bathroom they gather behind a screen to get a look and inadvertently knock it down. Bashō has produced a peculiar atmosphere, mingling earthy eroticism with rustic loneliness.

Kyorai senses the loneliness hidden in Bashō's lines and decides to enlarge it into a nature poem:

Yudono wa take no	On the bathroom floor,
Sunoko wabishiki	A modest bamboo mat.
Uikyō no	An evening storm
Mi o fukiotosu	Blows at the fennel plants
Yūarashi	And shakes down the seeds.

The scene is a large country house, probably a physician's. Outside the modest bathroom are a few fennels, which the owner planted for medicinal purposes. This particular evening a strong storm wind blows at the fennels and shakes down the seeds. As they fall they release a strong fragrance, which drifts into the bathroom. The refreshing feeling of taking a bath and the pleasant aroma of fennel seeds combine to create a uniquely harmonious mood.

The most fitting person for such a lonely evening scene would be a Buddhist monk in a gray robe slowly walking along a country lane. That is the picture Bonchō sees in his mind's eye:

Uikyō no	An evening storm
Mi o fukiotosu	Blows at the fennel plants
Yūarashi	And shakes down the seeds.
Sō yaya samuku	It's becoming cold–is that a monk
Tera ni kaeru ka	Returning to the monastery?

The monastery is probably located on top of a distant hill, and a lane is seen extending toward it in the evening twilight. The wind is blowing fiercely, fluttering the monk's gray robe. The whole scene is like a black-ink painting in the classical Chinese style.

Bashō who was fond of such a lonely atmosphere in the Chinese artistic tradition, gives it a subtle variation by introducing an apparently prosaic person, a showman who earns his livelihood by manipulating a monkey:

Sō yaya samuku	It's becoming cold–is that a monk
Tera ni kaeru ka	Returning to the monastery?
Saruhiki no	A monkey showman
Saru to yo o furu	And his monkey, together for years–
Aki no tsuki	The autumn moon.

The sudden appearance of this unlikely pair breaks into the lonely atmosphere and produces an almost humorous effect. Nonetheless, underneath the picture runs a feeling unmistakably forlorn. The showman is a lifelong wanderer; destitute and homeless, he roams from village to village begging for a few coins as his monkey performs its clever tricks before a small audience. His life is forever lonely; his only companion is the monkey. Bashō's last line, "The autumn moon," has the effect of symbolizing the showman's loneliness, which is basically the same as that of a Zen monk silently returning to his monastery.

Kyorai discards the Buddhist monk and brings the showman to the forefront:

Saruhiki no	A monkey showman
Saru to yo o furu	And his monkey, together for years—
Aki no tsuki	The autumn moon.
Nen ni itto no	Annually with a small amount of rice
Jishi hakaru nari	He pays his share of taxes.

In contemporary Japan a showman was among the lowest in social status. But this showman, although brought low by some misfortune, is honest and scrupulous. When harvest time comes round every autumn, he pays a small amount of rice to the government for his share of taxes. The poem at this point sketches the image of a well-ordered world where people lead peaceful lives, each in his own way.

Then the monkey showman disappears and there emerges a peasant's hut. Bonchō is responsible for the change:

Nen ni itto no	Annually with a small amount of rice
Jishi hakaru nari	He pays his share of taxes.
Goroppon	Five or six pieces
Namaki tsuketaru	Of freshly cut timber
Mizutamari	Over a muddy pool.

This is a scene often observed in swampy areas of rural Japan. The land is too marshy to be made into a farm, so it is left to waste. Across the edge of the swamp a few pieces of timber are laid down to walk on. Even in such a watery wilderness someone has settled; at the end of the lane stands a small hut, and the owner pays a tiny amount of tax each year. The harshness of his life is suggested by the image of freshly cut timber laid in the mud.

The next poet, Bashō, reinterprets Bonchō's lines and visualizes a muddy road on the outskirts of a town after a heavy rainfall:

Goroppon	Five or six pieces
Namaki tsuketaru	Of freshly cut timber
Mizutamari	Over a muddy pool.
Tabi fumiyogosu	The socks are spotted
Kuroboko no michi	With the black dirt of the road.

The severity of life has softened into the outline of a rather commonplace scene—a villager walking to town shortly after a rainfall. The occasion is a formal one; he is dressed in a new kimono, with a pair of white tabi on his feet. He has been walking carefully so that his socks will not get dirty, until his feet slip off the timber laid across a wet patch. A common little incident is made into poetry.

Naturally the reader starts wondering who this man could be. Kyorai thinks he is a sword-bearer—a page whose prime duty is to carry his master's sword:

Tabi fumiyogosu	The socks are spotted
Kuroboko no michi	With the black dirt of the road.
Oitatete	A sword-bearer on foot
Hayaki ouma no	Trying to catch up
Katanamochi	With the hurried master's horse.

The master has some urgent business to attend to, and without knowing it he hurries his horse. The sword-bearer falls behind even though he is walking as fast as he can, and of course the mud gets all over his feet.

The tension is comically relieved when Bonchō takes over:

Oitatete	A sword-bearer on foot
Hayaki ouma no	Trying to catch up
Katanamochi	With the hurried master's horse.
Detchi ga ninau	An apprentice boy carrying a bucket
Mizu koboshitari	Stumbles and spills the water.

The apprentice boy is just a passerby. As the samurai and his sword-bearer come hurrying along, the boy tries to step aside and let them pass, but in doing so he drops the bucket he is carrying and the water spills out. The poem has become quick-paced and comic, looking somewhat like a fragment of a story.

It is now time to subdue the fast, flamboyant rhythm. As usual, Bashō does so beautifully:

Detchi ga ninau	An apprentice boy carrying a bucket
Mizu koboshitari	Stumbles and spills the water.
To shōji mo	Doors and sliding screens
Mushiro-gakoi no	Are all covered with mats
Uriyashiki	At this mansion for sale.

The mansion is old and luxuriously built; the doors and sliding screens, like the rest of the house, show excellent workmanship, and in order to protect them from the elements and from vandalism the man selling the house has covered them with straw mats. As often is the case with such old mansions, there is a deep well in its yard with very good water, and the owner has kindly allowed the people of the neighborhood to use it. Now he is gone and the house is vacant, so this apprentice boy can help himself to the water without reserve. Here is a sharp contrast between the calm of the vacant old house and the flippancy of the boy who could not care less about the water he has spilled all around the unattended well.

Kyorai, the next poet, gazes at the old mansion and then turns his eyes toward its garden. Amidst the rampant grass there is something red:

To shōji mo	Doors and sliding screens
Mushiro-gakoi no	Are all covered with mats
Uriyashiki	At this mansion for sale.
Tenjōmamori	The pepper pods have turned red
Itsuka irozuku	With the passage of time.

Now the poem's theme is the effect of time. The owner, who enjoyed a luxurious living some time ago, has found himself powerless against the unpredictable hand of time; with the decline of his fortune, he has had to put his beautiful home up for sale. But time makes its mark not only on man but on all things in nature. In the neglected garden are a few pepper pods, which are slowly turning from green to red with approaching autumn, brightening the otherwise somber picture.

Now Bonchō imagines a new scene. The pepper pods belong in the vegetable garden in front of a peasant's hut:

Tenjōmamori	The pepper pods have turned red
Itsuka irozuku	With the passage of time.
Koso koso to	Noiselessly
Waraji o tsukuru	A straw sandal is braided
Tsukiyo-zashi	In the moonlight.

The autumn night is long, and the peasant cannot afford to waste it. Late at night he sits in front of the hut and braids a straw sandal, as farmers often do to help their family finances. He is working outside in order to save lamp oil; fortunately for him the moon is shining brightly. But he has to be cautious; he must not disturb his sleeping neighbors. Silently he keeps working all by himself, with only the pepper pods for company.

This rather dismal vignette of peasant life brightens with humor when Bashō adds a couple of lines:

Koso koso to	Noiselessly
Waraji o tsukuru	Straw sandal is braided
Tsukiyo-zashi	In the moonlight.
Nomi o furui ni	Someone comes out and shakes off
Okishi hatsuaki	The fleas into the early autumn night.

So the peasant's effort not to disturb his neighbors seems to have been in vain. Someone, probably a young man living next door, awakens and steps into the frontyard. But actually he has been awakened not by a noise but by fleas feasting on his body. He does not crush the fleas one by one with his fingers as an old woman might do; instead, he takes off his pajamas, brings them outside, and gives them a good shaking. Despite these details of a destitute peasant's life, the reader can almost feel the crisp autumn air and the bright moonlight.

Kyorai, amused by the picture of a man sleepily shaking fleas off his pajamas, responds with a triplet incorporating a similar mixture of humor and pathos:

Nomi o furui ni	Someone comes out and shakes off
Okishi hatsuaki	The fleas into the early autumn night.
Sono mama ni	A dry measure, set up
Korobi-ochitaru	To trap a mouse, falls to the ground
Masuotoshi	Without catching a thing.

Kyorai's lines refer to a mousetrap commonly used at the time. A large box-shaped measure is placed on the ground upside down, with a short stick slightly lifting it at one side. Inside is a small lump of food tied to one end of a string; the other end is attached to the supporting stick. As soon as a mouse bites at the food and pulls the string from the inside, the stick gives way and the measure falls over the mouse. Tonight, however, it is the mouse that is tricking the trapper; apparently the little animal has seen through the device and let the measure fall without being caught. The poor man is tortured by both mice and fleas!

Bonchō, also amused by the turn the renku is taking, keeps it going by adding another detail:

Sono mama ni	A dry measure, set up
Korobi-ochitaru	To trap a mouse, falls to the ground
Masuotoshi	Without catching a thing.
Yugamite futa no	The lid has been warped
Awanu hanbitsu	And no longer fits on the chest.

The mousetrap has been set up in a corner of the storeroom beside an old chest filled with all kinds of rubbish—outmoded clothes, broken utensils, chipped plates, old toys. The lid, warped with time, lies nearby. Dust, mildew, cobwebs and mouse droppings litter the room. The lines seem to point toward the beauty of the unrefined, the imperfect, the unharmonious. There is certainly something in common between a trap that has failed to catch a mouse and a chest whose lid does not fit. In both instances the poet contemplates the imperfect with a smile.

"The Summer Moon" is moving markedly in the direction of Bashō's later haiku. It is almost inevitable that Bashō, taking his turn, will visualize the image of a traveling poet just like himself:

Yugamite futa no	The lid has been warped
Awanu hanbitsu	And no longer fits on the chest.
Sōan ni	At a hermitage
Shibaraku ite wa	The man stays for a while
Uchiyaburi	And then takes off again.

With Bashō's poetic genius at work, Bonchō's couplet comes to assume a double meaning. At one level it is descriptive: the chest with a warped lid vividly exemplifies the way this hermit is enjoying a modest but carefree life. He does not wish to have new, splendid furniture; he has become a hermit precisely because he wants to escape from materialistic luxury. At another level, however, Bonchō's lines become symbolic. The lid that does not fit the chest suggests a man who does not fit into the world. He is a restless, homeless misfit; he wanders from one hermitage to another, never remaining anywhere for long.

It is natural that the next lines should follow up this traveling poet:

Sōan ni	At a hermitage
Shibaraku ite wa	The man stays for a while
Uchiyaburi	And then takes off again.
Inochi ureshiki	He is happy, living to an advanced age
Senjū no sata	And hearing about a new poetry anthology.

It is, of course, a great honor to have a poem included in an imperial anthology. The wandering poet, one day when he passed near the capital, was overjoyed to hear that some of his poems had been accepted by the compilers of a new anthology. He is happy that he has lived long enough to see the day when his poetry, for which he deserted everything else in the world, receives such an honor.

In passing we might note that this couplet was entirely different when Kyorai first made it up. In his original lines the reader could immediately identify the wandering bard as Priest Saigyō, the famous twelfth-century poet we met at the close of "A Winter Shower." Bashō, the team leader, did not like that obvious identification. He said, "It is all right to interpret the triplet as referring to the life of a poet like Saigyō or Nōin.[1] Yet it would be poor poetic craftsmanship if the lines following the triplet were directly related to a specific poet like Saigyō. The connecting link should be by means of 'shadow'." Here, then, Bashō seems to be insisting on the importance of ambiguity in poetry: a poet should not delineate his subject in detail, he should present only its "shadow," an indefinite form cast by the subject when it enters the poet's field of vision. Thus Bashō replaced Kyorai's couplet with the present one which, indeed, leaves the identity of the traveling poet ambiguous. The incident is one of many in which Bashō improved his disciples' verses.

The uncertainty about the bard's identity is immediately exploited by Bonchō, who transforms the wandering poet into an amorous courtier. Without Bashō's intervention, Bonchō could not have had the freedom to do so:

Inochi ureshiki	He is happy, living to an advanced age
Senjū no sata	And hearing about a new poetry anthology.
Sama zama ni	Various types of lovers
Shina kawaritaru	Who appeared in the past
Koi o shite	Are recalled to mind.

We might think of such a poet as Ariwara Narihira (825–80), the hero of *The Tales of Ise,* who is said to have had a wide variety of amorous adventures in his prime. Now an old man, long retired from all youthful activities, he hears one day that some of the love poems he wrote in his youth have been accepted for a new anthology. He is greatly pleased and brings out his old poetry notebook for the first time in years. As he reads the poems of his youth, he recalls his various sweethearts: one was a princess, another a courtesan, a third a young widow, yet another a minor official's wife, and so on.

With the image of an aged man recalling his youth, the poem inevitably comes to assume a Buddhist overtone. Bashō makes this clear in his couplet:

Sama zama ni	Various types of lovers
Shina kawaritaru	Who appeared in the past

Koi o shite	Are recalled to mind.
Ukiyo no hate wa	In this fleeting world, no one can escape
Mina Komachi nari	The destiny of that famed poetess, Komachi.

Ono Komachi was a beautiful and talented poet who lived in the ninth century. According to legends, she enjoyed a most proud and glorious youth amid a host of admirers, but as her beauty declined her life became very forlorn; it is said that she was even reduced to begging. The image of this aged lady introduces an element of pathos, the pathos that arises when graceful beauty is inexorably erased by time.

Kyorai gives this pathos a specific situation:

Ukiyo no hate wa	In this fleeting world, no one can escape
Mina Komachi nari	The destiny of that famed poetess, Komachi.
Nani yue zo	Why is it
Kayu susuru ni mo	That her eyes are filled with tears
Namida-gumi	Over a bowl of porridge?

The scene is probably a house at a rural village, to which this aged, shabbily dressed woman has come to beg for food. The kind master of the house gives her a bowl of porridge. Thanking him for his kindness, the beggar woman hungrily begins to eat. As he watches, the master notices tears welling up in her eyes and wonders why. Looking more carefully, he discovers in her features a lingering trace of her beauty and nobility. But he does not ask her about the past, and she does not volunteer an explanation.

Then Bonchō makes the beggar disappear; the mistress of a large house emerges:

Nani yue zo	Why is it
Kayu susuru ni mo	That her eyes are filled with tears
Namida-gumi	Over a bowl of porridge?
Orusu to nareba	How spacious the wooden floor looks
Hiroki itajiki	When the master is away from home!

In a Japanese house there is usually a wooden floor in the kitchen-dining area. In a large house it is a busy place, especially when the master is giving a party. In this house the energetic master is away on business, and his slender, frail wife is eating porridge all by herself. A maidservant, waiting on her, feels how bare and empty the dining area is. Then, by chance, she looks up and sees tears in her mistress's eyes.

Bashō builds upon Bonchō's lines. Instead of a maid waiting on her mistress at a meal, he visualizes a servant relaxing during his master's absence:

Orusu to nareba	How spacious the wooden floor looks
Hiroki itajiki	When the master is away from home!
Tenohira ni	Under cherry blossoms
Shirami hawasuru	A man watches a louse crawling
Hana no kage	On the palm of his hand.

The servant has no chores to do in the kitchen, or anywhere else for that matter, for his master is away. So he stretches out under a blossoming cherry tree in the garden, and watches a louse that has crawled out of his clothes onto the palm of his hand. The louse is enjoying the warm spring sunshine, and so is he. Here again Bashō has drastically changed the mood of the poem: the sad, even gloomy atmosphere that prevailed on the preceding verses has evaporated.

Kyorai chooses to replace the servant with a poet-recluse:

Tenohira ni	Under cherry blossoms
Shirami hawasuru	A man watches a louse crawling
Hana no kage	On the palm of his hand.
Kasumi ugokanu	Not a breeze to stir the thin haze,
Hiru no nemutasa	The drowsiness of a spring day . . .

Here is a person to whom the clamor of earthly life is entirely unknown. Having no ambition for material luxury or for worldly success, he spends a whole day under a blooming cherry tree, idly enjoying the beauty of springtime to his heart's content. When a louse crawls into his palm he watches it with a smile; when he becomes drowsy he takes a nap amid the fallen blossoms. It is in such a leisurely, peaceful mood that the renku at last comes to a close.

"The Summer Moon" was published in *The Monkey's Cloak* and has been widely read ever since as a model of Bashō-style renku. Here is the complete poem:

Natsu no Tsuki	The Summer Moon
Ichinaka wa *Mono no nioi ya* *Natsu no tsuki*	Above a town Filled with the odors of things, The summer moon.
Atsushi atsushi to *Kado kado no koe*	"It's hot!" "It's hot!" Murmurs are heard in the frontyards.
Nibangusa *Tori mo hatasazu* *Ho ni idete*	Though the second weeding Is not yet over, rice plants Shoot out their ears.
Hai uchitataku *Urume ichimai*	Ashes are brushed off a dried sardine Just taken from the fire.
Kono suji wa *Gin mo mishirazu* *Fujiyusa yo*	Those who live in this area Have never seen a silver coin. What a wretched place!
Tada tohyōshi ni *Nagaki wakizashi*	The fellow wears at his waist An absurdly long sword.
Kusamura ni *Kawazu kowagaru* *Yūmagure*	From the cluster of grass A frightening creature—a frog In the evening dusk.
Fuki no me tori ni *Ando yuri kesu*	The lady hunting for butterburs Jerks her lantern, and the light is gone.
Dōshin no *Okori wa hana no* *Tsubomu toki*	She set her mind On Nirvana, when cherry blossoms Were still in bud.

Noto no Nanao no
Fuyu wa sumi uki

At Nanao in Noto Province
It's hard to live through a wintertime.

Uo no hone
Shiwaburu made no
Oi o mite

A man, infirm
With age, slowly sucks
A fish bone.

Machibito ireshi
Komikado no kagi

He lets a lover in,
Unlocking the small gate.

Tachi kakari
Byōbu o tausu
Onago domo

The maidservants
Trying to take a peep
Knocks down the screen!

Yudono wa take no
Sunoko wabishiki

On the bathroom floor,
A modest bamboo mat.

Uikyō no
Mi o fukiotosu
Yūarashi

An evening storm
Blows at the fennel plants
And shakes down the seeds.

Sō yaya samuku
Tera ni kaeru ka

It's becoming cold–is that a monk
Returning to the monastery?

Saruhiki no
Saru to yo o furu
Aki no tsuki

A monkey showman
And his monkey, together for years–
The autumn moon.

Nen ni itto no
Jishi hakaru nari

Annually with a small amount of rice
He pays his share of taxes.

Goroppon
Namaki tsuketaru
Mizutamari

Five or six pieces
Of freshly cut timber
Over a muddy pool.

Tabi fumiyogosu
Kuroboko no michi

The socks are spotted
With the black dirt of the road.

Oitatete

A sword-bearer on foot

Hayaki ouma no *Katanamochi*	Trying to catch up With the hurried master's horse.
Detchi ga ninau *Mizu koboshitari*	An apprentice boy carrying a bucket Stumbles and spills the water.
To shōji mo *Mushiro-gakoi no* *Uriyashiki*	Doors and sliding screens Are all covered with mats At this mansion for sale.
Tenjōmamori *Itsuka irozuku*	The pepper pods have turned red With the passage of time.
Koso koso to *Waraji o tsukuru* *Tsukiyo-zashi*	Noiselessly A straw sandal is braided In the moonlight.
Nomi o furui ni *Okishi hatsuaki*	Someone comes out and shakes off The fleas into the early autumn night.
Sono mama ni *Korobi-ochitaru* *Masuotoshi*	A dry measure, set up To trap a mouse, falls to the ground Without catching a thing.
Yugamite futa no *Awanu hanbitsu*	The lid has been warped And no longer fits on the chest.
Sōan ni *Shibaraku ite wa* *Uchiyaburi*	At a hermitage The man stays for a while And then takes off again.
Inochi ureshiki *Senjū no sata*	He is happy, living to an advanced age And hearing about a new poetry anthology.
Sama zama ni *Shina kawaritaru* *Koi o shite*	Various types of lovers Who appeared in the past Are recalled to mind.

Ukiyo no hate wa	In this fleeting world, no one can escape
Mina Komachi nari	The destiny of that famed poetess, Komachi.
Nani yue zo	Why is it
Kayu susuru ni mo	That her eyes are filled with tears
Namida-gumi	Over a bowl of porridge?
Orusu to nareba	How spacious the wooden floor looks
Hiroki itajiki	When the master is away from home!
Tenohira ni	Under cherry blossoms
Shirami hawasuru	A man watches a louse crawling
Hana no kage	On the palm of his hand.
Kasumi ugokanu	Not a breeze to stir the thin haze,
Hiru no nemutasa	The drowsiness of a spring day . . .

If "A Winter Shower" is youthful poetry, "The Summer Moon" displays the features of a renku composed by a team of more mature and relaxed poets. It is less tense, less dramatic and less novel, because the scenes it presents are closer to those encountered in ordinary life. Where the first group tried to encompass the whole range of widely varying human lives, the second concentrated on probing into qualities basic to the experience of common men. Inevitably, some of the verses in "The Summer Moon" point toward sabi, toward the loneliness of living in this world with all our human limitations. Indeed, such images as a monk returning to his monastery on a cold evening, a showman alone with his monkey under the autumn moon, and pepper pods slowly turning red in the yard of a vacant house, have much in common with Bashō's later haiku. Furthermore, other verses seem to suggest a way by which this loneliness might be overcome. The lonely, gloomy scenes are overlaid by pictures of lighthearted humor. The dismal sketch of an impoverished peasant is brightened by the humorous picture of a young man shaking fleas out of his pajamas, and the loneliness of a tearful wife eating porridge in an empty kitchen is somewhat relieved by the suggestion that a happy life can be enjoyed by anyone willing to forsake the petty conventions of society. Such verses have the flavor of "lightness" that permeates some of the haiku of Bashō's last years.

This confirms, then, that Bashō's growth as a renku writer was along much the same lines as his evolution as a haiku poet. And that is only natural. It must be conceded, however, that the evidence of his growth is clearer in the haiku than the renku because, as has been observed, the latter's form imposes many more limitations on the poet. In writing a haiku Bashō could be completely himself, but he had to think of his teammates when he composed a verse for a renku, even though as the leader he must have had considerable power to influence their verses. Still, the renku gave greater play to at least one aspect of Bashō's creative genius than the haiku. They show the depth and scope of his poetic imagination more clearly than any other literary form in which he wrote. By its very nature, a renku verse need not be based on the poet's actual experience; he can conjure up a scene solely from his imagination. Reading "A Winter Shower" and "The Summer Moon" we realize how penetrating and far-reaching Bashō's imaginative power was, and how enjoyable it must have been for him to roam in the world of fancy while composing a renku. And he was not alone in that world of dreams; his teammates usually found it, too, under his guidance. In this respect he was a happy poet, for he was blessed with a host of disciples who were only too willing to follow him in his endless wandering.

CHAPTER 4

Prose

BASHŌ was an accomplished prose writer. Anyone writing a history of Japanese prose literature will have to include him, for he virtually created a new prose style which became a model for many writers in succeeding generations. In writing prose, Bashō exerted the same meticulous care as he did in composing a haiku or a renku verse, and he wanted his students to do the same. He once planned to compile a prose anthology from his and his disciples' work, but he was forced to abandon the plan when he found there were too few pieces that met his standards. Such a serious concern for perfection in prose style had not been common in Japan before his time. For one thing, Bashō apparently thought of prose and poetry as complementary, as two modes of writing serving a single aim. Certainly one of the main charms of Bashō's prose lies in its poetic beauty, in the way poetry is brought into prose. In such a work as *The Narrow Road to the Deep North,* the ordinary distinction between poetry and prose almost disappears.

Bashō's works in prose fall into three groups: *haibun,* travel journals, and critical commentaries. Haibun can be said to be haiku prose, or prose written in the spirit of haiku. When it is applied to Bashō's works the term usually refers to short occasional prose pieces involving the same sort of topics and viewpoints as his haiku. Bashō's travel journals are five in all: *The Records of a Weather-Exposed Skeleton, A Visit to the Kashima Shrine, The Records of a Travel-Worn Satchel, A Visit to Sarashina Village,* and *The Narrow Road to the Deep North.* To these we should add *The Saga Diary,* which was written during one of his journeys and contains some features common to the other journals. Critical commentaries are found in *The Seashell Game* and a few lesser-known manuscripts, as well as in many of his disciples' works which record his informal conversations.

These are very interesting in that they reveal Bashō's views about poets, poetry, and poetics. In this chapter we shall treat only the first two groups, leaving the third to the next chapter.

I *The Haibun: Haiku in Prose*

Today's Japanese scholars disagree as to the exact number of Bashō's haibun, partly because some of them take into account the short headnotes to many of his haiku. For our purpose, we shall exclude headnotes and treat only the longer and more independent pieces, numbering between sixty and seventy. Still, they vary considerably in length: "An Essay on the Unreal Dwelling" ("Genjū-an no Ki"), the longest, contains nearly fifteen hundred words in Japanese, while the shortest pieces barely exceed one hundred. Yet they share several features. One of the most conspicuous is that many end with one or more haiku. The prose sections leading up to the final haiku generally show a common structural pattern in pieces dealing with similar subjects. The subjects themselves fall into several general categories; they do not show too wide a range.

As can be expected of a person who spent much of his life traveling, a considerable number of Bashō's haibun are about the places he visited. Generally speaking, in one of these pieces he briefly introduces the locale, goes on to give his thoughts about it, and concludes with a haiku. For instance, here is his haibun on Matsushima, one of the most scenic places in Japan, which he visited during his journey to the far north:

Matsushima boasts of having the most beautiful view in Japan. Poets have focused their attention on this island scenery since ancient times, expending on it their best efforts in literary craftsmanship. The bay is about three leagues in diameter, and the islands of many shapes that float on it show the wonders of a supreme artistry possessed only by nature. With pine trees growing densely on each island, the landscape has a colorful beauty that is beyond description.

Shima-jima ya	All those islands!
Chiji ni kudakete	Broken into thousands of pieces,
Natsu no umi	The summer sea.

Though it is not described, we can well imagine the bright summer sun glittering over the blue Pacific. The vast expanse of the ocean is limited by the arms of the bay and by the scattering of small islands. But even the way the great expanse is limited is on a grand scale. Here once more we have the image of a poet faced with the beauty and infinity of nature, and that confrontation is implicit in both the prose and the haiku.

A haibun belonging to the same category but with a more personal feeling is a short piece on the House of Fallen Persimmons, written when Bashō was staying there in 1691:

A man named Kyorai, who lives in Kyoto, has a cottage among the bamboo bushes in lower Saga, at the foot of Mount Arashi and close to the Ōi River. It is a convenient place for one who seeks loneliness, for it is precisely the type of place that calms one's mind. Kyorai is a lazy man: by the windows weeds grow tall, and several persimmon trees are left free to stretch their branches over the roof. As summer rains have been leaking everywhere, the tatami floor and the sliding screens smell of mildew, and it is not at all easy even to pick a spot to sleep at night. For me, however, the shadiness of the place has become a sign of the hospitality of the host.

Samidare ya	The seasonal rain—
Shikishi hegitaru	Poetry cards have been peeled off,
Kabe no ato	Leaving traces on the wall.

This cottage, the House of Fallen Persimmons, is said to have originally been a noted tea master's residence. The esthetics of the tea ceremony centered on the beauty of shade, spareness, and asymmetry as against that of brightness, plenitude, and symmetry. Bashō's predilection was of course for the former type of beauty, and this haibun shows his thorough enjoyment of it in his quiet life there. A poetry card is a small square card designed specifically for writing a poem on to be presented to someone as a gift. Bashō, sitting alone in the cottage and listening to the early summer rain, suddenly notices several square marks on the wall beside him. He decides they must be the traces of poetry cards which a former occupant, no doubt a lover of poetry, peeled off when he moved out. The incessant sound of rain and the image of the poetry cards which are no longer on the wall merge in the poet's mind.

These are only two of many haibun by Bashō that tell of places. What accounts for this fascination? Naturally, different places had different attractions; Matsushima with its gorgeous beauty, and Saga with its plainness, equally attracted him. One interesting fact is that wherever he might be he always thought of the past, of the people who had once lived or visited there. At Matsushima he thought of bygone poets who had sung of the beauty of the island scenery; at Saga he pondered the lover of poetry who had lived in the same cottage. Bashō visited various places to commune with the memory of those with whom he felt he shared the same attitude toward life. Though they were dead and gone, the surroundings were imbued with their presence and gave inspiration to the sensitive visitor.

It goes without saying that Bashō also liked to meet *living* people who shared his interest in poetry and in things poetic, and these people are central to the second group of his haibun. These pieces, too, are similar in structural pattern. Typically they begin with a brief introduction of an individual, explain his present circumstances, and go on to point out some characteristic that brings him closer to the writer. They often end with a haiku dedicated to the subject. A good example is a short prose piece on Sora, which was given in its entirety in our first chapter. Another example is on Ochi Etsujin (1656?–1739), Bashō's favorite traveling companion in 1680s:

Jūzō, a resident of Owari Province, has the pseudonym Etsujin. It was derived from the name of the area where he was born. He lives amid the bustle of town, but this is merely to earn a livelihood. Whenever he has worked for two days he takes the next two days off; if he has toiled for three days, he spends the following three days amusing himself. He is a born drinker, and when he is drunk he sings medieval ballads. He is my friend.

Futari mishi	Together we two enjoyed
Yuki wa kotoshi mo	Watching the snow—I wonder
Furikeru ka	If it has snowed this year, too.

The sentences are short, and the style is rather terse, yet the warmth of congenial friendship flows underneath. In the haiku Bashō is recalling the winter of 1687, when he and Etsujin undertook a short journey to the Pacific coast. In referring to their snow-viewing during that trip, Bashō is implying that he and Etsujin share the same poetic taste, which is the solid foundation of their friendship.

Bashō's concept of the ideal haiku poet is even better reflected in another haibun that falls in the same category. This piece was written in the summer of 1693, when his disciple Morikawa Kyoroku (1656–1715) was leaving for his home province on official business:

The man returning to his native place by way of the Kiso road is named Morikawa Kyoroku. Since ancient times, those with a feeling for poetry did not mind carrying satchels on their backs, or putting straw sandals on their feet, or wearing humble hats that barely protected them from the elements. They took delight in disciplining their minds through such hardship and thereby attaining a knowledge of the true nature of things. Now, Kyoroku is a samurai who serves his lord and his country. He wears a long sword at his waist and rides on a post horse; a spear-bearer and a page attend him on the road, their black garments fluttering in the wind. I am certain, however, that such an appearance is not indicative of his true self.

Shii no hana no	Be like the heart
Kokoro ni mo niyo	Of those pasania blossoms
Kiso no tabi	As you travel the Kiso road.

Uki hito no	Follow the footsteps
Tabi ni mo narae	Of those pensive travelers
Kiso no hae	Amid the flies of Kiso.

The Kiso road, which threads through the mountainous areas of central Honshu, was rugged and desolate; a man traveling there would feel especially lonesome when he walked under tiny pasania blossoms or spent a night at a rustic inn where flies are rampant. Bashō was telling his disciple that such an undertaking would provide a good opportunity to discipline the poetic mind. Kyoroku being one of his newer students, Bashō was direct and frank in stating his idea of a true poet's life. The two haiku at the end (Bashō asked Kyoroku to choose one, but his disciple preferred to retain both) are unusually didactic for Bashō.

Bashō wrote a number of other haibun about specific persons, and from them emerges a man quite unlike the lonely poet: a warm friend, an understanding teacher, a gentle, likable person indeed. He had, however, a discriminating taste in choosing a friend or a student; the person had to be a true poet at heart, one who was perceptive of the beauty of nature, sensitive to both the loneliness and the humor in human life, and indifferent to material luxury. Bashō was genuinely delighted to meet such a person, and that was at least part of the reason why he went traveling so often.

Yet the haibun that reveal Bashō's thoughts and feelings most clearly are those of the third group, the ones that deal with specific things and events. Drawing directly on actual occurrences, they are snippets of his outer and inner life, scattered fragments of his diary. It is difficult to find a general structural pattern in them. Some begin with a description of the event in question, then present the writer's reaction to it, and conclude with a haiku. Others start off with a general statement on human life or nature and go on to a discussion of the writer's own life in the light of that statement, concluding with a haiku. For example, here is a haibun Bashō wrote in the autumn of 1690:

Unchiku, a monk living in Kyoto, once painted what appeared to be a self-portrait. It was a picture of a monk with his face turned away. Unchiku showed me the portrait and asked me to write a legend for it. I said, "You are more than sixty years of age, and I am nearing fifty. We are both in a world of dreams, and this portrait depicts a man in a dream, too." Then I jotted down a sleeper's talk beside the portrait:

Kochira muke	Will you turn toward me?
Ware mo sabishiki	I am lonely, too,
Aki no kure	This autumn evening.

Unchiku (1630–1703) was an artist and is said to have been Bashō's teacher of calligraphy. This haibun is interesting in that it reveals the basis of Bashō's friendship with him, and probably with many others as well. The poet saw all men as lonely and helpless in this world of illusions, and he wanted paradoxically to make that loneliness the basic bond between himself and others. The haiku has a playful overtone, but beneath lies the deep solitude characteristic of Bashō's later poetry.

The following haibun also reveals Bashō's underlying attitude toward life. It was written in the autumn of 1692, when banana trees had just been transplanted into the garden of the third Bashō Hut:

Admirable is a person who has nothing that hampers his mind. Laudable is a man devoid of worldly talent or knowledge. The same can be said of a homeless wanderer, too. Yet, leading such a totally liberated life requires an iron will, a willpower so strong that it can hardly be contained in a person resembling a weak-winged dove.[1] At one time, as if caught by a sudden whirlwind, I dashed out on a journey to the north and roamed about with a tattered hat on my head. Three years later I was back again to the east of the river in Edo where, sorrowfully gazing at the water that flowed in two different streams[2] on an autumn day, I shed nostalgic tears over yellow chrysanthemum flowers.[3] Then my disciples Sanpū and Kifū built this new hut for me out of the kindness of their hearts, and it has since been tastefully furnished, too, by the help of Sora and Taisui who love beautiful simplicity.[4] Facing south, the hut can withstand both winter cold and summer heat. At the edge of the pond are bamboo railings, no doubt for the convenience of a moon-viewer. Indeed, I become restless in fear of rain and clouds every nightfall, even when the moon is yet in its early phases. People give me all kinds of things to enhance my enjoyment of life here; they keep my gourd filled with rice, and my bottle filled with rice wine. Though the hut is hidden fairly deep among the trees and bamboos, they have now planted five banana trees to make the view of the moon even more beautiful. The banana leaves are more than seven feet long and could cover a koto or be made into a bag to keep a biwa in.[5] In the wind they flutter like a phoenix's tail feathers, and in the rain they are torn like a green dragon's ears. The rolled new leaves grow day by day as in Master Heng-ch'ü's theory of learning; they readily unroll, as if waiting for Saint Shao-nien's brush. Unlike those two men, however, I derive no use from my banana plants. I simply enjoy their shade; I love those leaves that are so easily torn by the wind and the rain.

Bashō-ba o	Banana leaves will be
Hashira ni kaken	Hanging near the pillars—
Io no tsuki	Moon-viewing at my hut.

Master Heng-ch'ü refers to Chang Tsai, a neo-Confucian scholar of Sung times who once wrote in a poem that he wished his knowledge would grow as fast as new banana leaves. Saint Shao-nien, also known as Huai Su, was a master calligrapher of T'ang times who practiced calligraphy on banana leaves when he was young and poor. They were highly gifted men, and Bashō respected them both. Yet he found himself unable to follow in their footsteps, because neo-Confucianism and calligraphy were "worldly knowledge" and "worldly talent" that hampered the mind. Bashō's ultimate aim was liberation from all things, philosophy and the arts included. However, he was humble enough to recognize this was a goal beyond attainment, and he was too warm-hearted to reject the kindness of his well-meaning disciples, who wanted their master to live in comfort. He therefore decided to live contentedly in the world of common men while keeping his ideals high above theirs. In a style typical of haibun, this prose piece reveals Bashō's way of life in his later years. The haiku at the end is a meaningful one when read in this light.

Bashō's longest haibun, "An Essay on the Unreal Dwelling," also has a confessional nature. One of the finest haibun of all time, it displays Bashō's prose craftsmanship at its best. He rewrote it several times, each time carefully scrutinizing and revising the previous draft.[6] On one occasion he even asked Kyorai and Kyorai's brother to read and improve on it. As its title indicates, the haibun tells of Bashō's life at the so-called Unreal Hut near Lake Biwa in the summer of 1690. The final draft was probably completed in the autumn of that year, shortly before he left the mountain hideout.

The essay has a tight, well-ordered structure. It begins with a brief introduction of the locale. The opening sentences state that the hut is situated halfway up a mountain, deep in a wooded area. They also mention a Buddhist temple which had stood there in the remote past, and a Shinto shrine which still stands in the vicinity; these references deepen the feeling of isolation from ordinary town life. The passage goes on to an explanation of whence the hut derived its name: it was originally owned by a monk whose Buddhist name was Genjū ("unreal"). The monk, of course, has long been dead.

After establishing the secluded nature of the location, the

haibun comes to focus on the writer's own life in the previous decade. Here Bashō compares himself to a bagworm that has lost its bag and to a snail that has left its shell. He was homeless, he says; he had wandered through the country, most recently in that rugged journey to the far north. He then came to the shores of Lake Biwa and settled in this hut in the summer of 1690. This part of the haibun ends with a confession that the author has become very fond of the place.

The third section, the main body of the essay, is a description of Bashō's life at the Unreal Hut which makes clear why he likes staying there. First of all, he explains, he enjoys the beauty of nature, adorned with azaleas, wistarias, cuckoos, and jays. Secondly, he can admire scenic views to his heart's content; he can look at beautiful Lake Biwa and some shapely mountains near it in the distance. The area is replete with historic sites that evoke various poetic associations in the sensitive onlooker's mind; by contemplating those distant views the poet revives distant memories. Thirdly, he can indulge in a free, leisurely way of life without interruption. Liberated from all social obligations, he can take a nap whenever he is sleepy; he can cook a meal whenever he feels hungry. In the daytime he may listen to a farmer talking about some incidents on the farm; at night he may wander alone in the moonlight, sunk in random thoughts.

Having thus described his daily life at the hut, Bashō now turns his attention to his inner feelings. The fourth and final part of the essay is a passage of introspection:

All this, however, does not mean that I am an avid lover of solitude who wishes to hide in the mountains once and for all. I am more like a sickly person who has retired from society after becoming a little weary of mixing with people. As I look back over the many years of my frivolous life, I remember at one time I coveted an official post with a tenure of land and at another time I was anxious to confine myself within the walls of a monastery. Yet I kept aimlessly wandering on like a cloud in the wind, all the while laboring to capture the beauty of flowers and birds. In fact, that finally became the source of my livelihood; with no other talent or ability to resort to, I merely clung to that thin line. It was for the sake of poetry that Po Chü-i tired himself out and Tu Fu grew lean.[7] I am saying this not because I regard myself as an equal of those two Chinese masters in wisdom and in poetic genius. It is because I believe there is no place in this world that is not an unreal dwelling. I abandoned the line of thinking at this point and went to sleep.

Mazu tanomu	My temporary shelter,
Shii no ki mo ari	A pasania tree is here, too,
Natsu-kodachi	In the summer grove.

The passage is the focal point of "An Essay on the Unreal Dwelling"; it is related to all three preceding parts in a way that gives each a new meaning. In the introductory part Bashō talked about Genjū, the Buddhist monk who built the hut; he has now established himself as a rightful heir to the founder. Then he referred to his years of wandering in rather derogatory terms (bagworm and snail), yet now he has justified them. In the third part he described the joys of living at the Unreal Hut; he has now explained what they derive from. In his youth Bashō wavered among various possible courses of life ranging from the most utilitarian (a government post) to the most spiritual (monastic life). From all the possibilities, however, he chose what he had to choose: the life of a bird that soars in the boundless sky singing of the beauty of nature. Of course the bird has to rest somewhere once in a while, perhaps atop a towering pasania tree, no matter how briefly. The final haiku has an ambiguity typical of Bashō: it may be about a bird perching in a pasania tree, or about a poet resting in the Unreal Hut, or about men in general having a short respite in this ever-changing world.

In concluding our discussion of Bashō's haibun we shall consider the question: What distinguishes a haibun from an ordinary essay? One answer that comes readily to mind is that a haibun usually (though not necessarily) ends with a haiku. The implication is that a haibun is a perfect prose complement to the haiku. As we have said, the word haibun means haiku prose, a prose piece written in the spirit of haiku. The essential qualities of haiku are seen in the haibun in their prose equivalents, as it were.

A haibun has, for instance, the same sort of brevity and conciseness as a haiku. It is very short, in many cases between one hundred and fifty and two hundred and fifty words in Japanese. Because of this brevity, the writer is as concise as possible, avoiding unnecessary words; in fact, he often omits words that would be necessary in normal syntax. Although this is not evident in English translation, the predicate verb of a sentence is sometimes left out, leaving the reader to supply it by himself. Another stylistic feature is a deliberately ambiguous use of certain particles and verb forms in places where the conjunction "and" would be used in English. Just as many haiku juxtapose two disparate objects without explicitly stating the relationship, a haibun occasionally incorporates two phrases or clauses connected by an ambiguous "and," leaving the reader to interpret it. Sometimes even this "and" is omitted, so that the two phrases hang without any obvious connecting link. The reader must "leap" from one phrase to the other in his imagination. Take, for example, two sentences from the haibun on Etsujin: "He is a born drinker, and when he is drunk he sings medieval ballads. He is my friend." In the first sentence the meaning of "and" is a little ambiguous. And there is a bigger "leap" between the two sentences, though there is no connecting word. "He is my friend" has a forceful effect as a consequence. The lack of a connecting word between phrases, clauses, and sentences is undoubtedly more conspicuous in Japanese, a language attached to conjunctions.

The same can be said of the relationship between the prose part of a haibun and the haiku that follows. Bashō never explains the meaning of his haiku; he just places it at the end of the haibun, usually without any connecting words. It is up to the reader to grasp the meaning of the prose, and then of the haiku, and to go on to discover the undercurrents of meaning common to both. Furthermore, by ending in a haiku the whole haibun leaves the reader with a feeling of incompleteness. This can be compared to the structure of many a haiku, where the third line is verbless and grammatically cut off from the first two lines. Just as such a haiku sets the reader's mind busily working to complete the third line, a haibun concluding with a haiku will expand in the reader's imagination after he finishes reading it. The poet, especially in the haiku, often deliberately avoids the tone of finality that normally sounds in prose.

Another characteristic of the haibun is the extent of its dependence on imagery. To be sure, literary Japanese prose has always tended to be imagistic rather than logical in all genres, but Bashō's haibun carry that tendency to an extreme. Abstract, general, conceptual words are shunned in favor of concrete visual images. Bashō uses the expression "weak-winged dove" instead of "weak-willed man," or talks of "capturing the beauty of flowers and birds" instead of "writing poetry," or says "I was back again to the east of the river in Edo where, sorrowfully gazing at the water that flowed in two different streams on an autumn day, I shed nostalgic tears over yellow chrysanthemum flowers" instead of "I returned to Edo one autumn day." The main advantage of using decorative language like this is, of course, its emotive effect. A sentence impregnated with images extends the borders of the reader's imagination, because it is not intellectualized. Bashō's sentences, especially in his later works, are short and rich in imagery, with conjunctions at a minimum.

As might be expected, two types of images predominate in Bashō's haibun: nature images and classical images. Many nature images are of flowers, plants, birds, and animals with which he was familiar, and he used them with ease as vehicles of his emotional expression. His pseudonym, Bashō, is itself an evocative nature image. Classical images create associative effects; they lead the reader to see the passage in the light of Japanese or Chinese classics. The image of a weak-winged dove invites the initiated reader to recall a passage in a certain Taoist classic in which an ignorant dove laughs at a phoenix; that of a man shedding tears over yellow chrysanthemums asks him to ponder Tu Fu's poem on autumn.

Naturally Bashō's haibun make abundant use of Chinese characters, which are ideograms and therefore have visual appeal. Japanese characters, which are phonetic symbols, are often omitted in his haibun even where they would normally be used, or are replaced by Chinese characters. The frequent occurrence of Chinese characters has the effect of shortening sentences, for one Chinese ideogram will often stand for two or more Japanese characters. This also helps to make a haibun short, even though it is so in appearance only.

Lastly, we might mention the writer's detachment as a characteristic of haibun. No good haibun is an emotional outburst or logical persuasion. The writer, standing back from his subject matter, coolly examines his feelings and casually records them.

In the last passage of "An Essay on the Unreal Dwelling" Bashō may seem emotionally involved, but at the last moment he withdraws from that involvement and says, "I abandoned the line of thinking at this point and went to sleep." The haibun about Etsujin and on Kyorai were actually given to those two men respectively, but Bashō refers to them in the third person instead of the second, seeing his relationship with them from an objective point of view. Sometimes a writer's detachment permits a little humor. Certainly Bashō was in a playful mood when he called out to a portrait and asked it to turn its face toward him. He was lighthearted, too, when he talked about the difficulty of picking a spot to sleep in the House of Fallen Persimmons, or when he compared a banana leaf to a phoenix's tail and to a dragon's ear. Unquestionably, such touches of humor are related to the idea of "lightness" found in Bashō's later haiku. We have again returned to our starting point: the haibun is a prose equivalent of haiku.

II *Journals: Records of a Wandering Heart*

Bashō's journals closely resemble his haibun. All but one being travel journals, they contain passages that treat the places he visited, the people he encountered, and the events he came across, in the same manner and style as haibun. In several instances a passage is so similar in style and subject matter to a haibun that the one is thought to be a different version of the other: the haibun on Matsushima, for example, appears to be a draft of the section on Matsushima in *The Narrow Road to the Deep North,* and the last paragraph of "an Essay on the Unreal Dwelling" seems to be a polished version of the opening passage of *The Records of a Travel-Worn Satchel.* As far as prose style is concerned, it is impossible to distinguish between a haibun and a journal; in this regard Bashō's journals can be, and sometimes are, called haibun.

Yet journals do differ from ordinary haibun in one obvious and important respect: they are usually longer and comprise a number of passages, each of which might have been a haibun by itself. These haibun-like passages, each with its own theme, mood, and tone, have been put together in such a manner that they present a single but complex comment on life. In this respect the relationship of a haibun to a journal can be compared to that of a haiku to a renku. Just as we enjoy the varying moods of the verses that make up a renku, so we take delight in the changing feelings of a traveler as we follow him from one place to another in his journal. And, just as there is a coherent progression through the verses of a renku, there is a prevailing set of themes and tones that unifies the parts of a journal. This should be so, because to qualify as a work of literature a journal must be unified by something of more consequence than a mere sequence of dates.

Bashō's first literary journal, *The Records of a Weather-Exposed Skeleton,* came out of his long westward journey of 1684–85, which took him to a dozen provinces lying between Edo and Kyoto. As literature it has a number of imperfections that reflect his inexperience in writing a journal. The prose does not have the density of texture and refinement of style of his later journals. The haiku that are scattered through the prose retain, in varying degrees, the traces of his more experimental early poetry. Moreover, the prose and poetry do not always maintain a harmonious and balanced relationship. Frequently a prose passage functions merely as a headnote to the haiku that follows; this is expecially true in the second half, where in many cases the headnote is reduced to one or two lines. Seen as a whole, the journal is noticeably deficient in proportion.

The Records of a Weather-Exposed Skeleton, however, does have a dominant theme which runs consistently beneath its uneven surface. The theme can be termed a search for enlightenment: How could a man, doomed to live through a continual strife with himself and others, attain perfect peace of mind? This was in fact Bashō's prime aim in undertaking the journey. It is expressly stated in the opening passage:

People in the good old days set out on a long journey without packing provisions for the road, and yet they are said to have entered a realm of perfect liberation under the moon late at night. Leaning on the staff of those travelers, I left my dilapidated hut on the riverside in the eighth month of the first year of Jōkyō, when the autumn wind was blowing with an unaccountably chilling sound.

Nozarashi o	A weather-exposed skeleton
Kokoro ni kaze no	Haunts my mind: how the wind
Shimu mi kana	Penetrates my body!

Bashō, increasingly aware of the pains of living, wished to enter "a realm of perfect liberation" by any means possible. One way suggested by men of old was to travel—to go on a journey with all its hazards, that of death included. Bashō decided to take up this suggestion, but to do so he had to face the possibility of his own death. He saw in his mind's eye his own skeleton lost in the wilderness and beaten by rain and snow. Knowing it all, he still dared it. If the haiku sounds a bit conceited, that is because a pseudo-heroic pose was needed for his confrontation with the possibility of death. He was not yet ready for death, so he had to strike a deliberately resolute posture in facing it.

Also, as has been pointed out, travel in seventeenth-century Japan was a far more risky undertaking than it is now. In fact, Bashō saw someone confronted with death soon after he took to the road. In an oft-quoted passage from *The Records of a Weather-Exposed Skeleton* he writes:

On a road along the Fuji River we came upon an abandoned child, about two years of age and crying pathetically. Apparently his parents, finding the waves of this floating world as uncontrollable as the turbulent rapids of this river, had decided to leave him there until his life vanished like a dewdrop. He looked like a tiny bush-clover blossom that would fall any time tonight or tomorrow beneath the blow of an autumn gust. I tossed him some food from my sleeve pocket, and mused as I passed by:

Saru o kiku hito	Poets who sang of monkey's wailing:
Sutego ni aki no	How would they feel about this child forsaken
Kaze ika ni	In the autumn wind?

How did this happen? Were you hated by your father, or were you shunned by your mother? No, your father did not hate you, nor did your mother shun you. All this has been Heaven's will; you have nothing but your ill fate to grieve for.

In this instance, Bashō resolved the problem by resorting to determinism. There are many cruelties in this world, and sometimes a human being has to lose his life in an unreasonable, inhuman way. Yet all this is Heaven's will; there is nothing we can do about it, except resign ourselves to it. Bashō, while knowing that he had to surrender to this truth in the end, must have felt quite depressed about it. His hyperpathetic tone and sentimental imagery seem to suggest a conscious effort to subdue the part of his inner self that resisted surrender to fatalism. The haiku, consisting of nineteen syllables instead of seventeen, also seems to indicate that the poet's emotion was overflowing.

Another instance where Bashō vented intense and unresolved emotion, recorded a little later in the journal, occurred when he returned to his birthplace and was shown a tuft of his dead mother's hair. As has been mentioned, Bashō wrote the following haiku:

Te ni toraba	Should I hold it in my hand
Kien namida zo atsuki	It would melt in my burning tears—
Aki no shimo	Autumnal frost.

Again the abnormal 5-9-5 syllable pattern suggests an uncontrollable intensity of emotion. But this poem contains an element not found in the previous two haiku, a hint that Bashō was beginning to find the direction toward a resolution. The key image is autumnal frost. In his mind's eye Bashō transformed a tuft of his mother's gray hair into autumn frost, and by doing so he could submerge his personal grief in a more universal sadness. He could look at his grief more objectively, and therefore more calmly, by imagining that the tuft of hair was frost, part of ever-changing nature.

Other incidents recorded in *The Records of a Weather-Exposed Skeleton* substantiate Bashō's gradual growth. One of them, which took place in the first part of the journey, resulted in a haiku we saw earlier:

Michinobe no	Blooming by the lane
Mukuge wa uma ni	A rose mallow—and it has been
Kuwarekeri	Devoured by the horse!

Ambiguous as the poem is, there seems to be little doubt that the poet felt a measure of affinity with the rose mallow. But an incident that reveals the nature of Bashō's growth more distinctly is recorded near the halfway mark in the journal. He was then visiting a Zen temple near Nara, when he saw an ancient pine tree:

Sō asagao	Priests and morning-glories:
Iku shinikaeru	How many generations of them
Nori no matsu	Under the pine of the Law!

This is probably too didactic to be considered a fine poem; indeed, it could be called a hymn. Again Bashō was too emotionally involved with the occasion to compose a good poem. Its very imperfection seems to indicate his impatient search for a resolution.

The second half of *The Records of a Weather-Exposed Skeleton* begins to show some results of Bashō's quest for peace of mind. He no longer strikes that heroic, grandiose pose, nor does he wail in a hyperpathetic voice. He is calmer; he can regard himself from a certain distance. In fact he even looks back to his exaggerated stance and writes a few lines:

When I came to Ōgaki I stayed at Bokuin's house.[8] I recalled how the image of a weather-beaten skeleton had haunted my mind at the time of my departure from Musashi Plain.[9]

Shini mo senu	I am not yet dead
Tabine no hate yo	After many nights on the road–
Aki no kure	End of an autumn day.

We can imagine Bashō smiling a little when he showed this haiku to Bokuin that night. This sort of objectification of the self and a light humor resulting from it are also noticeable in a haiku that appears several passages later:

Kyōku	*A Comic Poem*
Kogarashi no	In the wintry gust,
Mi wa Chikusai ni	A wanderer: how like Chikusai
Nitaru kana	I have become!

Chikusai, the hero of a popular contemporary tale, was a quack doctor who wandered through various provinces while writing comic poems on the way. Bashō takes pleasure in comparing himself to Chikusai; he is enjoying the life of a wanderer now.

It is not difficult to anticipate that the journal will end quite differently from the way it started. *The Records of a Weather-Exposed Skeleton* comes to a close with this short passage:

Toward the end of the fourth month I returned to my hut and recuperated from the fatigue of the journey.

Natsugoromo	My summer robe–
Imada shirami o	There are still some lice
Toritsukusazu	I have not caught.

It had taken nine months to complete this long journey, during which Bashō went through a wide variety of new experiences, some of them not easy to bear. The hardships left marks on him as lice do on one's body, and once back home he could recognize them. What he should do now was recall those trying episodes one by one, re-experience them in calm recollection and then put them away in writing. It would be a refreshing and spiritually enriching task which could restore him from exhaustion. The concluding haiku beautifully presents a double image–a weary traveler hunting down lice on his robe after a long journey, and a poet recalling his emotion in tranquility after a series of new experiences. The hyperpathetic note with which the journal began is no longer here at the end. Instead there is a touch of humor: hardships of travel have been transformed into lice. In the Japanese literary tradition a louse was not necessarily a detestable creature; as we saw at the close of "The Summer Moon," it often provided companionship for a poet-recluse who loved to spend his leisure hours in quiet musing.

Bashō's next journal, *A Visit to the Kashima Shrine*, is much shorter. The journey itself was short: it is only fifty miles or so from Edo to Kashima, and he was on the road only for a few days. The journal also differs from *The Records of a Weather-Exposed Skeleton* in its structure, for its first half is a prose description of the trip, and its second half consists of poems which Bashō and others composed in and near Kashima. The structure can be likened to that of an ordinary haibun in which a short prose piece is rounded off by one or more haiku.

The principal motif of *A Visit to the Kashima Shrine* is esthetic: an appreciation of the beauty of nature, and through it, union with past poets. The express purpose of the jaunt was to see the harvest moon at Kashima in the scenic lake country. "I decided to go and see the harvest moon at Kashima this autumn, after fondly recalling a similar thing an ancient poet did . . ." writes Bashō in the opening sentence. As it happened, Bashō passed several scenic places on the way. At Kamagai he saw Mount Tsukuba towering above the wide expanse of the plain and remembered an ancient poem about it; at the fishing village of Fusa he recalled a travelling Chinese poet who sang of a fishy smell floating into his bedroom one night. And at his destination Bashō was deeply moved by the beauty of the landscape even though the weather was most unfavorable. In the climactic passage of the journal he writes:

Beginning in the afternoon, showers came frequently. The moon did not seem likely to appear that evening. I had heard that the former priest of Konpon Temple was living a secluded life at the foot of the hill, so I sought out his residence and spent the night there. Like that Chinese poet[10] who was led into deep meditation at a temple, I felt as if I attained serenity of mind for a time during that evening. Toward dawn the sky cleared a little. I awakened the priest, and others who were there got up, too. There was the moonlight, there was the sound of rain—the beauty of the scene so overwhelmed my mind, I was left without a word to say. How sorry I felt, having come such a long way to see the moon and then failing to write a worthy poem there! But I also remembered that famed lady:[11] even she could not produce a poem on cuckoos at one time and went through a good deal of anguish upon returning home empty-handed. I might say she provided good companionship for me that evening.

The esthetic aim, with which Bashō began the journal, is pushed to an extreme in this final prose passage. The ultimate in beauty cannot be described; it lies beyond the means of the artist. But he need not be disheartened by this, because he is, after all, a witness and participant. He may not be able to depict the scene in word or in pigment, but he can absorb it in his mind. Poetry is not merely an art of expression but a spiritual discipline. It is significant that Bashō chose to see the harvest moon with a Zen priest. As Zen holds that its ultimate secrets are inexpressible in words, Bashō realizes that ultimate visual beauty in nature is indescribable.

The poetry section that follows includes eight haiku by Bashō, six haiku by his two companions, one tanka by the retired Zen priest, and the first three verses of a renku with Bashō participating. Characteristic of Bashō's eight haiku is an objective, impersonal quality; the impassioned, often pathetic tone found in the early poems of *The Records of a Weather-Exposed Skeleton* is gone, and the poet, rather than projecting his emotion into his poem, presents a scene of nature which he watches calmly. For instance:

Tsuki hayashi *Kozue wa ame o* *Mochinagara*	The moon fleeting fast, Foliage atop the trees Holds the rain.
Shizu no ko ya *Ine surikakete* *Tsuki o miru*	A peasant's child Husking the rice, pauses To look at the moon.
Imo no ha ya *Tsuki matsu sato no* *Yakebatake*	Taro leaves— In the village awaiting the moonrise, A parched farm.

These haiku, all of them about the harvest moon, catch the beauty of nature in its various manifestations. The poet is an admirer of natural beauty, a passive but sensitive agent who alertly responds to various aspects of the beauty of nature. The stormy moon above the rain-soaked woods, the rustic moon shining down on a peasant's child, the imagined moon over a parched farm—Bashō can enjoy the beauty of them all. These haiku complement his esthetic stance in the prose section.

The Records of a Travel-Worn Satchel, the third of Bashō's travel journals, records the first half of his long westward journey in 1687–88. Longer than the first two, it traces Bashō's footsteps as he leaves his riverside home in Edo, travels along the Pacific coastline and reaches his native Ueno. It continues as Bashō pays short visits to noted places in that area, such as Mount Yoshino, Mount Kōya, Wakanoura, Nara and Suma, and ends with his visit to Akashi, the farthest point west on his itinerary. In recording his experiences, *The Records of a Travel-Worn Satchel* follows the structural method of *The Records of a*

Weather-Exposed Skeleton. Its form is as if a number of short haibun, many of them ending with one or more haiku, were strung together in chronological order. In terms of prose style the journal is closer to *A Visit to the Kashima Shrine*, with relatively restrained language and subdued imagery.

The Records of a Travel-Worn Satchel, however, differs markedly from the earlier journals in that the writer is more consciously ideological. Bashō no longer gropes around among different ways of living; he has chosen one and is directing the course of his life accordingly. This he makes amply clear at the outset. In the openng passage, which is in its implications much like the last paragraph of "An Essay on the Unreal Dwelling," he recalls how undecided he once was about his future and how he finally came to choose poetry as his profession. Then, in a more didactic tone rarely found in his earlier prose, Bashō goes on to write:

> One thing permeates Saigyō's tanka, Sōgi's linked verse, Sesshū's painting and Rikyū's tea ceremony.[12] That is the spirit of the artist who follows nature and befriends the four seasons. Everything he sees becomes a flower, and everything he imagines turns into a moon. One who does not see the flower is akin to a barbarian, and one who does not imagine the moon is no different from a beast. Leave barbarians and beasts behind. Follow nature and return to nature.

This is in substance an extension and theorization of the estheticism suggested in *A Visit to the Kashima Shrine*. Appreciation of beauty in nature is not only a way of softening man's griefs, but the very basis on which man is differentiated from a beast; it is the basis of civilization. The degree to which a person can appreciate beauty in nature determines the degree of his culture; the more of an artist he is, the more civilized he is. This is because an artist, by perceiving beauty in nature, is able to come closer to the Creator. Bashō's stand is that of an esthetic primitivist, and hence his plea "Return to nature." That is the central theme of *The Records of a Travel-Worn Satchel.*

Still in a theorizing mood, Bashō then goes on to make clear his views on the art of writing a travel journal:

> The habit of writing a travel journal began with Tsurayuki, Chōmei and the nun Abutsu, who expressed all sorts of poetic sentiments in beautiful passages.[13] Their followers' works, however, all look imita-

tive and fall short of improving on the models. Far less gifted, I never expect my writing to match the ancient masterpieces. Anyone can write that on such and such a day it was rainy in the morning and cleared in the afternoon, that a pine tree stood at such and such a place, or that such and such a river flowed through such and such a district. Indeed, it is not worthwhile writing a journal unless there is something new to say, as in the poems of Huang Shan-ku or Su Tung-p'o.[14] Nevertheless I must say the scenes I came upon during the journey still remain in my memory and the hardships I encountered still provide a topic of conversation today. A record of these will help me to return to nature. With this thought in mind, I have here patched together some passages that record the especially memorable moments of my journey. I hope my readers will forgive me for doing this, considering it nothing more than a drunkard's raving or a sleeper's muttering.

Beneath the characteristic tone of modesty we can detect Bashō's firm confidence in what he is doing. He is doing something new in the journal, something never undertaken even by famed writers like Tsurayuki and Abutsu. He is recording the journey of a man who has consciously attempted to return to nature, of a poet who has tried to follow nature and to befriend the four seasons. Anyone with poetic inclinations will be helped in his attempts to return to nature when he reads the journal; to others the journal will seem nothing more than a drunkard's raving or a sleeper's muttering.

The rest of *The Records of a Travel-Worn Satchel*, which in the main describes occurrences along the road, reflects Bashō's firm belief in this type of esthetic primitivism. There are several segments that clearly suggest his effort to approach the Creator by means of submersion within an object of nature. For example, here is a haiku he composed on his visit to the Grand Shinto Shrines at Ise:

Nan no ki no	From which tree's bloom
Hana to wa shirazu	It comes, I do not know:
Nioi kana	This fragrance!

A faint fragrance fills the holy precincts, and the poet cannot tell which tree it is coming from. Kneeling before the shrines and smelling that fragrance for some time, he is drawn into an illusion that it is emanating from the mysterious world of ancient gods. Another interesting haiku that appears a little further on is:

Nao mitashi	All the more I wish to see
Hana ni akeyuku	Among those blossoms at dawn
Kami no kao	The face of the god.

The god, enshrined at a temple on Mount Kazuraki near Nara, was popularly believed to have a very ugly face. But the poet, who approaches the deity by means of immersion in nature, cannot be convinced of this because the natural world surrounding the temple is so beautiful. He wonders whether the popular belief may not be wrong, and he yearns to see the deity's face even more eagerly than before.

The following haiku, composed when Bashō visited a ruined temple at Awa in Iga Province, suggests that he actually saw Buddha:

Jōroku ni	A holy image, sixteen feet high–
Kagerō takashi	Shimmering heat waves rise
Ishi no ue	From the stone foundation.

In the prose passage preceding the haiku Bashō makes clear that there was nothing on the weather-beaten stone foundation, for the image of Buddha had long been torn down. What the poet saw was just shimmering heat waves, one of the manifestations of nature's life-force; but, gazing at them intently, he could see the thin air gradually taking the shape of Buddha's image.

Of course, *The Records of a Travel-Worn Satchel* includes many other haiku and prose passages dealing with more occasional topics. It cannot be denied, however, that the Bashō who emerges out of it is on the whole a happier, more confident, and more carefree man than ever before. The journal contains several poems of a playfulness seldom found in the other journals. Here is one written in Nagoya after a snowfall:

Iza yukan	Let's walk around
Yukimi ni korobu	To enjoy the scenes of snow
Tokoro made	Until I slip and fall!

Another was composed on the New Year's Day when he overslept and could not join the early morning festivities:

Futsuka ni mo	On the Second Day
Nukari wa seji na	I'll be more careful–
Hana no haru	Flowering spring.

These are not very serious compositions; Bashō was not feeling very serious. Nevertheless he chose to record them in the journal, no doubt because they faithfully rendered his jovial mood on those occasions.

Next in the series, *A Visit to Sarashina Village,* is the shortest of all Bashō's journals. Like the brief *A Visit to the Kashima Shrine,* it has a structure similar to a haibun: the first half in prose, and the second half in verse. Likewise, the aim of the trip was to see the harvest moon at a rustic place, and the journal centers on that theme. "A desire to go and see the harvest moon at Mount Obasute in Sarashina Village grew stronger in me each time the autumn wind blew . . ." begins the journal. Bashō's two travel companions are then introduced: his friend Etsujin and an attendant lent to him by his disciple Kakei. A glum-looking Buddhist monk joins the group a little later. The main body of the journal focuses on the ruggedness of the road, an unpredictable road which now becomes a steep slope, now crosses a deep valley, now looks over turbulent rapids. The prose portion concludes with a scene in which Bashō enjoys a lovely view of the moon at an inn in Sarashina. The remainder consist of thirteen haiku written during the trip, eleven by Bashō and two by Etsujin.

We wonder what prompted Bashō to write this short journal. *The Records of a Travel-Worn Satchel* covered his journey of 1687–88 up to Akashi; he then stopped writing even though he kept on traveling. Presumably Bashō felt he could add nothing new; he felt if he went on writing he might sink to the level of ordinary journal writers who merely imitated Tsurayuki and Abutsu. Why, then, did he choose to write *A Visit to Sarashina Village* when he was aware of all this?

The answer must be that Bashō did have something new to say, something he had not said in *The Records of a Travel-Worn*

Satchel. This is most clearly suggested at the end of the prose section, in the climactic passage of the journal:

While my attention was distracted by other things the moon had risen beyond the trees, and its rays began filtering through the broken wall. The sounds of wooden clappers and the calls of deer hunters were heard far and near. The pensive mood of autumn had never been so keenly felt. "Now," I said to my companions, "let me offer some rice wine to you moon-viewers." With that the innkeeper brought out wine cups, which were noticeably larger than ordinary ones and bore rather crude designs in gold lacquer. Though a resident of the capital would think them unrefined and would not even touch them, I was fascinated by those cups against all expectation; I felt as if they were priceless bowls adorned with radiant gems. This too was because of the locale.

The locale, Sarashina, was different from areas Bashō had visited before: primitive, untamed nature was still preserved there. It gave fresh stimulation to the poet, so much so that he could discover beauty in things he had previously thought too crude. With the tenet "Return to nature" Bashō had traveled far and wide, but always in predominantly civilized areas, unaware that he had not "returned" to the deepest heart of nature. He probably felt a bit embarrassed when he thought of the high-flown words with which he declared the purpose of his pilgrimage at the outset of *The Records of a Travel-Worn Satchel.* It was not necessary to take them back, for they represented one stage of his growth; but he must have felt obliged to add a few words somewhere to indicate he had left that stage behind. This was at least part of his motive for writing *A Visit to Sarashina Village.* Without doubt it was a principal motive for his long journey to the far north a little later.

This frame of mind is also reflected in one of the eleven poems he wrote for the second half of *A Visit to Sarashina Village.* The haiku reads:

Kiso no tochi	Chestnuts of Kiso—
Ukiyo no hito no	My souvenirs to those
Miyage kana	In the floating world.

These chestnuts are not of an ordinary variety; they are only found deep in the mountains, for example in Kiso Province where Sarashina is located. Unlike ordinary chestnuts they are not very tasty; in fact, to be edible they have to be cooked. It is obvious, then, that they symbolize wild, untouched nature seldom glimpsed by those who are busy pursuing their pleasures in the "floating world." Bashō is implying that the haiku and prose passages written during this journey, artless and crude as they may seem, are rare gifts to those accustomed to more urbane literature. He wanted to introduce the charms of the wilderness to a wider audience.

It comes as no surprise, then, that Bashō's next journey was to the most undeveloped part of Japan and that the resulting journal was called *The Narrow Road to the Deep North.* The "narrow road" in the title is more metaphorical than literal, and so is the "deep north." On the surface the journal, by far the longest of Bashō's works in this genre, records the events of his journey of 1689 to the northern part of Honshu. Yet at the metaphorical level it is a record of Bashō's spiritual quest, a quest for the ultimate beauty of nature and of man which had been lost in the contemporary "floating world." The journal appropriately comes to its close when Bashō reaches Ōgaki and is surrounded by a host of admirers. He has reached the floating world there; he no longer finds sense in continuing the journal.

Thus *The Narrow Road to the Deep North* abounds with descriptions of people and things whose unobtrusive beauty is rarely found outside of rugged, primitive nature. For instance, this passage appears early in the journal:

In the shade of a large chestnut tree near this post town, a Buddhist monk was living a secluded life. It seemed a quiet life, indeed, like that of an ancient poet-recluse who picked horse chestnuts in the depths of the mountains. I wrote down on a piece of paper: "The Chinese ideogram Chestnut consists of two letters that signify West and Tree respectively. Hence Bodhisattva Gyōki[15] is said to have associated a chestnut tree with Western Paradise and used it both for his cane and for the pillars of his house.

Yo no hito no	Few in this world
Mitsukenu hana ya	Notice those blossoms:
Noki no kuri	Chestnut by the eaves.

The poem can be interpreted literally and metaphorically. Chestnut blossoms are small and unostentatious, and bloom in the rainy season; they are an apt metaphor for the life of this retired monk. "This world" in the poem means the floating world. The haiku recalls the chestnuts of Kiso we saw in the poem at the end of *A Visit to Sarashina Village*.

Another early passage praises an individual keeping his distance from the floating world. This man is not a monk; he is an innkeeper living amidst the people:

On the thirtieth day we stopped at the foot of Mount Nikkō. The master of the inn we stayed at said, "I am called Buddha Gozaemon. People honor me with this name because I try to be honest in everything I do. So please make yourselves at home and have a good rest tonight." That set me to wondering what sort of Buddha he could be to reveal himself in this earthly mire and to help beggarly pilgrims like ourselves. I watched the innkeeper closely and found him a ruggedly honest man who had no worldly wisdom or shrewdness. Confucius once remarked that a man of sturdy simple mind approaches Perfect Virtue. Such innate purity as this innkeeper's should be most highly valued.

Instead of wildly primitive nature here is a stubbornly honest man, the sort rarely found in an urban, sophisticated society. He is artless, almost naïve; he can tell his guests he is called Buddha, without suspecting that they may consider him presumptuous. Bashō suspected and watched him closely; he found in him not a Buddha but the sort of man so simplehearted as to precede both Buddhism and Confucianism. Bashō saw an image of primeval man unspoiled by the evils of civilization.

Of course, not all the people Bashō encountered were like these two people. Inevitably, some were unenlightened and earthy. But to write about them would be of no help to the presentation of the central theme; better to omit them althogether. This is precisely what Bashō did. According to Sora, who accompanied Bashō and who wrote his own more factual diary, Bashō was entertained by high-ranking samurai and well-to-do merchants at various towns. When he was in Sakata, for instance, he was given hospitality by one of the wealthiest merchants in that commercial city on the coast of the Sea of Japan. In Murakami, a town near Sakata, he was invited to the castle of a local lord and was presented with a substantial amount of money. In Kashiwazaki, another town on the coast, he visited a millionaire's mansion for an overnight stay, but he was somehow treated discourteously and left at once, though it was raining and people at the mansion rushed out to stop him. These people and events would have been memorable enough for the average person to record in his diary, if he kept a diary at all. Bashō makes no mention of them whatsoever. *The Narrow Road to the Deep North* is a literary journal with a deliberate choice of facts.

Not only did Bashō freely choose to omit material, but he changed the facts as he saw fit. *The Narrow Road to the Deep North* is fictional to some degree. The purpose is again the same: Bashō wanted to present his theme more effectively. The following, for instance, describes what occurred when Bashō and Sora left Matsushima:

> On the twelfth day, we set out for Hiraizumi. Having heard that such famous places as the pine of Aneha and the bridge of Odae were near, we chose to take a lonely path that only hunters and woodcutters would use. But soon we lost our way completely and stepped onto the wrong trail, and eventually we found ourselves at a harbor called Ishinomaki. Kinkazan, the island where an ancient poem says flowers of gold blossomed,[16] was seen far out on the sea. In the bay hundreds of barges were anchored, and on the shore numerous houses were clustered, from which the smoke of cooking rose incessantly. We had never expected to come to a town like this! We sought a place to stay for the night, but no one was willing to offer us one. We ended up spending the night at a bleak little house. Next day we again continued to wander along a road totally unknown to us. Looking at the ford of Sode, the meadow of Obuchi and the heath of Mano in the distance, we traveled over an embankment that stretched endlessly. We then plodded along a long marsh in a desolate area, finally coming to a place named Toima. After a night's stay there, we arrived at Hiraizumi. I think we had covered more than twenty leagues by then.

The passage successfully conveys the lonely, helpless feeling of the two travelers who blundered into a remote area completely unknown to them. It also dramatizes their unexpected joy upon coming to Ishinomaki and its vicinity, which were famous in classical poetry. But the truth seems to be that Bashō and Sora never lost their way. The pine of Aneha and the bridge of Odae were located to the west of Matsushima, and Ishinomaki was to the east; it is highly unlikely that such experienced travelers would unknowingly take a road to Ishinomaki when they intended to reach Aneha and Odae. Sora's diary makes no mention of their getting lost here; it sounds as if they had planned to go to Ishinomaki from the beginning. As a matter of fact, Ishinomaki is frequently mentioned in an itinerary Sora had prepared for Bashō before the whole journey began. Furthermore, Bashō's words "We sought a place to stay for the night, but no one was willing to offer us one" are not true to the facts. A kind person Bashō and Sora met on the way guided them to an inn (not "a bleak little house") in Ishinomaki; they had no difficulty finding accommodations there. The sentence "Next day we again continued to wander along a road totally unknown to us" is not quite factual either, for in reality two Ishinomaki residents, who must have known the road very well, accompanied them as they left.

There are similar instances elsewhere in *The Narrow Road to the Deep North*. To mention just a few, at Iizuka the journal says that Bashō had a severe attack of his chronic illness and almost fainted, but Sora's diary, which is especially detailed on that day, has no record of it. In Matsushima Bashō's journal implies he was too overwhelmed by the beautiful scenery to compose a poem; yet, as we have seen, he did write a haiku. In Kisagata the journal states: "That morning the sky was very clear. When the bright morning sun came out, we went boating on the sea." Yet Sora's diary confirms that it drizzled all that morning, and that they went boat riding only after supper. To explain these discrepancies, it may be argued that Bashō's memory of events had become fuzzy by the time he wrote the journal. That may be true in some cases, but Bashō's alterations of fact point too uniformly in one direction to be attributed to mere failure of memory. In almost every case they beautify and dramatize the writer's experience in that lonely pilgrimage through the rugged north. The writer seems more interested in giving us the same sort of spiritual experience than in the prosaic recording of facts. This is expected of any literary journal. Though to a lesser degree, Bashō did it in his earlier journals.

And he was not original here, either. Ancient Japanese court diaries, beginning with Tsurayuki's, were fictional to varying degrees. Many of them seemed to be based on the assumption that it was more important to record inner experience than outward events.

It does not surprise us, then, that for Bashō this was an exploration not only in space but also in time. While he traveled through the wild north and met sturdy unsophisticated men, he also wandered into a bygone age and had imaginary talks with its inhabitants. In some passages of *The Narrow Road to the Deep North* he minimizes description of a place in order to write more about the past event connected with the place. The following was written on the occasion of his visit to a Shinto shrine near Kanazawa:

We visited Tada Shrine here and saw Sanemori's helmet as well as a remnant of the robe he wore under his armor. According to the legend, these had been given him by Lord Yoshitomo, his master in his youth. Indeed, they did not look like an ordinary soldier's. The helmet was inlaid with an arabesque of gold chrysanthemums from the frontlet to the ear-plates, with a dragon's head and two curved horns adorning the crown. The legend vividly told how after Sanemori was killed the enemy general Kiso Yoshinaka sent his deputy Higuchi Jirō to this shrine to offer a letter of prayer along with these mementoes.

Muzan ya na	How pitiful!
Kabuto no shita no	Underneath the helmet
Kirigirisu	A cricket chirping.

Sanemori was a heroic warrior of medieval times who appears in several masterpieces of Japanese literature, including a nō play by that name. When more than seventy years of age, after dyeing his gray hair black, he fought his last battle among an army of young soldiers. Gazing at the helmet and brocade robe on display at the shrine, Bashō wanders into the twelfth century, a century of war and disorder which demanded the utmost heroism from every person of integrity. Sanemori was a samurai who lived heroically and died heroically; in his own way he too proceeded along the "narrow road to the deep north." The first line of Bashō's haiku, "How pitiful!", is taken from the nō play *Sanemori*, and refers not only to the mournful chirp of an autumn cricket but also to the aged samurai's last battle. It is pitiful and ennobling to see the warrior following the course of his destiny with determination and courage.

Such excursions into the past occur throughout *The Narrow Road to the Deep North.* The passage about Yashima, a place near Nikkō, dwells on the legend of a mythological princess who dared to stay in a burning house to prove her chastity to her husband. In the section on Hiraizumi Bashō mainly reminisces about the glory it enjoyed in the twelfth century. In Shiogoshi, a village some distance west of Kanazawa, he leaves out the scenery altogether, preferring to quote a tanka which Priest Saigyō had written when he was there several centuries earlier. Reading through all these passages we get the impression that Bashō was just as interested in meeting the ghosts of men who had lived there long ago as in meeting his contemporaries. In this sense the writer of *The Narrow Road to the Deep North* can be compared to the deuteragonist of the nō drama, in many cases an itinerant monk who invokes the ghost of a past local resident wherever he goes. Bashō, traveling not only geographically but also historically, is a medium who conjures up bygone persons and events for his readers. And, of course, these visions point in one direction: they all reveal the beauty and sadness of primitive nature and of premodern men steadfastly following their courses of life.

As the language of the nō play must necessarily be poetic and evocative in order to help the audience visualize a world beyond the tomb, the language of *The Narrow Road to the Deep North* is concise, allusive, and figurative to induce the reader to share the author's experiences, actual and emotional. The passages are loaded with sensory images. Most of the sentences are short and crisp, seldom with a conjunction between them. Occasionally two more or less unrelated phrases or clauses are juxtaposed, connected by nothing more than a nominal "and." Often a haiku appears in the middle or at the end of a prose passage, without much explanation but with perfect emotional logic. In brief, the language of *The Narrow Road to the Deep North* has the same qualities as Bashō's finest haibun. The journal can be described as a collection of about fifty superb haibun.

The "leap" method used in haibun seems to have been developed into a structural method unifying the whole journal. On the surface, the structural unity of *The Narrow Road to the Deep North* is attained chronologically: passages describing places and people are arranged in the order in which Bashō visited them. Yet, as we have seen, he took a good deal of liberty in the choice of what and whom he wrote about. While the primary criterion of choice was thematic, the author also seems to have considered structural factors. In selecting material, he carefully studied the nature of each passage and tried to make its successor harmonious and complementary. As a consequence, between two passages which apparently are contiguous because of the time sequence, a "leap" occurs.

To mention just a few examples, early in the journal a passage on Yashima is followed by a paragraph on Mount Nikkō. The first is the one about a mythological princess who braved fire to prove her chastity; the latter is that about an innkeeper who is nicknamed Buddha in praise of his integrity. Though Bashō gives not a word of explanation, we involuntarily make a "leap" from one passage to the other as we read them. Likewise, the passages about Hiraizumi which present the poet standing among the desolate ruins and recalling the town's past prosperity are preceded by a section that describes him plodding through a lonely woodland and arriving at a thriving harbor town called Ishinomaki. A passage on Kanazawa tells of Kosugi Isshō (1653–88), a young man devoted to the art of poetry who had died the previous winter; it is followed by the paragraph on Sanemori, the aged warrior who courageously followed the medieval samurai codes and was killed in a manner befitting a young soldier.

Some Japanese scholars have argued that *The Narrow Road to the Deep North* has the structure of a renku. Judging by these samples, we must say the argument has a measure of validity. Just as two consecutive verses in a renku are related in a uniquely poetic way, two consecutive passages in this journal work on each other and establish a theme or mood of their own—a theme or mood that is somewhat modified when a third passage is added. The fifty-odd haibun that constitute *The Narrow Road to the Deep North* are built on such an apparently casual but unobtrusively coherent structure. Of course this does not mean they lack variety. As members of a renku team consciously attempt to include a wide range of subjects such as nature, town life, love, religion, travel and so on, so Bashō in his journal now describes a beautiful scene on the northern seacoast, now writes of an interesting man he met, and now turns to express reverence for a diety enshrined at a place he visited. He even sees to it at times that women and children add a bit of color to the largely somber beauty of the north. The most effective of these passages occurs toward the end of the journal when he, after a hard day of trekking along the northern coast, meets two young courtesans at his inn:

Hitotsuya ni	Under the same roof
Yūjo mo netari	Courtesans, too, are asleep—
Hagi to tsuki	Bush clover and the moon.

Whether Bashō was deliberately using the renku technique is, of course, irrelevant. *The Narrow Road to the Deep North* does have unity in variety, and variety in unity, qualities that have contributed to its lasting reputation as one of the finest literary journals Japan has ever produced.

After the travel described in *The Narrow Road to the Deep North,* Bashō stayed at the homes of various friends and disciples around Kyoto, Nara, and Lake Biwa. One of the most enjoyable of these sojourns was at Kyorai's cottage in Saga, the House of Fallen Persimmons. *The Saga Diary* is Bashō's own record of his fifteen days there. It cannot therefore be classified as an ordinary travel journal in which the writer moves from one place to another day by day. Where in Bashō's previous journals dates are mentioned in a rather casual manner, in this diary the date is meticulously recorded. In fact, each section of the diary is headed by a date, as in the case of an ordinary diary.

In other respects, however, *The Saga Diary* differs from an ordinary diary and shows some traits peculiar to Bashō's travel journals. To begin with, it makes amply clear that the writer is a traveler; it is a traveler's diary even though he is staying at one place. He does make two short excursions during the fifteen days: to visit a Buddhist temple and see an imperial concubine's grave, and to view the summer landscapes from aboard a boat on a nearby river. The diary also describes what might be called imaginary journeys: one rainy morning he ponders Saigyō's life and recites his poems, and one night he dreams of his beloved disciple Tokoku who had died the previous year. Furthermore, we read that news is frequently brought to him in letters and by visitors: one disciple in Edo writes about his recent visit to the old Bashō Hut, and another disciple pays his master a visit and talks about his blossom-viewing trip to Mount Yoshino. According to the diary, Bashō had visitors almost every day: Kyorai, Sora, Bonchō and his wife, a samurai, a Buddhist monk—all visited him one after another. In effect it was almost like traveling. Bashō used to travel in order to meet different people; here in Saga, different people come and meet him.

Most important, *The Saga Diary* resembles Bashō's travel journals in its theme. The central theme is suggested in its opening paragraph, the entry under the eighteenth of the fourth month. After a brief description of the location of the cottage and his room in it, the passage concludes: "I forget my poverty and enjoy a serene, leisurely life here." The diary is a substantiation of this statement; it tells what a serene, leisurely life is like. All the events that occur at the cottage can be considered different phases of that life. The writer is probably in the happiest phase when he stands outside the cottage and composes the haiku:

Te o uteba	I clap my hands
Kodama ni akuru	And with the echoes, it begins to dawn—
Natsu no tsuki	The summer moon.

He is more quiet and solemn when in the dead of night he contemplates a nearby bamboo bush and composes the haiku:

Hototogisu	The cuckoo—
Ōtakeyabu o	Through the dense bamboo grove,
Moru tsukiyo	Moonlight seeping.

In a phase dramatic and sad, and yet not without humor, he stands before the grave of an imperial concubine who committed suicide in the twelfth century:

Uki fushi ya	A sorrowful destiny–
Take no ko to naru	Man turns into a bamboo shoot
Hito no hate	At his inevitable end.

The concubine's grave was in a bamboo bush where many young shoots were then appearing. That inescapable fact of life, death, is here referred to in connection with a bamboo shoot, quite a familiar food item in Japan. The poet has attained such serenity that even when he visualizes the pitiful destiny of a lovely lady he can gaze at it with calm sympathy. This kind of peace and calm underlies all the phases of the diarist's life at the cottage.

Written with such an aim in the author's mind, *The Saga Diary* is a work of literature based on a single theme, not merely a record of events at a certain house at a certain time. Indeed Bashō attempted to be selective in recording events, concentrating on those that present the theme most effectively. He also endeavored to maintain a structural unity: the opening passages are written in a formal, slow-paced prose; the middle section covers a variety of topics in a free mixture of prose and poetry; and the final part resumes a calmer tone, altogether following the structural principle of a renku in a very general way. Yet apparently the diary was not left to us in its final form. We do not know whether Bashō did not complete his revisions or whether the final draft was lost. But whatever the reason, *The Saga Diary* is somewhat lacking in the density of texture, refinement of style, and delicate sense of proportion that are so beautifully blended in *The Narrow Road to the Deep North.*

CHAPTER 5

Critical Commentaries

BASHŌ was always deeply interested in the work of other poets. In a way this was inevitable, because in his day no haikai poet worked in complete isolation. A renku had to be composed by a team of poets; its very existence depended upon enthusiastic cooperation. A haiku, too, was often written in the presence of other poets, or was sent to one as a message or greeting, or was shown to others for evaluation and criticism. There was also the haiku contest, in which poems were paired in rivalry. Under such circumstances, each poet's critical consciousness could not but deepen. Bashō, in addition, was a professional teacher of poetry; day after day he had to evaluate his students' verses and to suggest ways they could be improved. Judging from the available evidence, he seems to have been a very good teacher, a sincere, perceptive, and constructive critic whose judgment could be relied upon and whose comments were always inspiring. It would not be amiss to assume that many gifted young poets became his students not merely because he was a famed poet but because he was such an excellent critic. And they were not wrong in this assessment; by today's standards, Bashō is without doubt a major figure in the history of Japanese literary esthetics.

Bashō, however, wrote no elaborate treatise on the art of poetry. A haikai poet, he instinctively shied away from abstraction and systematization. Therefore his critical attitudes can be glimpsed only indirectly, through casual comments scattered in his haibun and journals, through critical remarks about specific works of poetry, and through informal conversations with his students. This makes it very difficult for us to formulate his theory of poetry without oversimplification. In the following pages, then, we shall not try to present a neatly systematized Bashō poetic; rather, we shall go directly to representative examples of his commentaries and see what sort of critical attitudes lie beneath them.

I *Early Haiku Contests*

Bashō's first work of literary criticism, *The Seashell Game* (1672), has the honor of being his earliest known book as well as the only one he published in his own name.[1] It concerns a poetry contest which matches sixty haiku in pairs, reminiscent of the way Japanese girls pair seashells in the seashell game. Of these haiku, two are declared to be Bashō's, and the remaining fifty-eight are attributed to thirty-six other poets. Very little is known about most of these poets; they were most likely amateurs in or near Ueno, or in some cases might have been fictional poets created by Bashō to disguise his own authorship. At any rate, the verses are not of a very high quality; by and large the themes are trite, the tone frivolous, and the material often vulgar. They are, however, peculiarly uniform in their language: they clearly reflect the language of the common people, especially of fashionable young townsmen who frequented gay quarters and who took pride in the witty use of the slang, popular songs, and clichés then in vogue. Interestingly enough, young Bashō attempted to use the same sort of language in his critical commentaries, and in this he was marvelously successful. As a result, *The Seashell Game* produces a singularly uniform impression: it is a collection of town sophisticates' poems commented on by another town sophisticate for the amusement of knowledgeable readers.

The following is an example of Bashō's critical judgment in *The Seashell Game*. It is the twenty-second round of the contest, a match between two haiku on the subject of colorful autumn leaves.

Toriyagebaba ga *Migi no te nari no* *Momiji kana*	How like it is to A midwife's right hand— Crimson maple leaf!	*Sanboku*
Momijinu to *Kite miyo kashi no* *Eda no tsuyu*	"I haven't crimsoned. Come and look!" So says the dew On an oak branch.	*Dasoku*

Autumn leaves were the subject of many a graceful poem in old Japanese court literature. Obviously Sanboku's poem derives its interest from presenting a shocking variation on the theme: a vivid maple leaf is compared to the bloody hand of a midwife. Dasoku's poem, on the other hand, is about a Japanese evergreen oak tree. Standing out against its neighbors' tinted leaves and covered with white dew, the oak appears quite confident of its attractiveness. Furthermore, the oak uses a cliché from popular songs of the time: "Come and look!"

Now Bashō, in judging Sanboku's poem to be the winner, made the following comment:

> The first poem employs a unique conceit in dealing with the subject of colored leaves. The second is well said, but it shows the poet to be a man of queer tastes: he likes a colorless oak tree and has no liking for the world of colors. The first poem suggests, with its lines about a midwife's red right hand, that the poet is well versed both in the art of love and in the skill of giving birth to vigorous language. It ranks thousands of leagues above the second poem. Therefore, if invited to come and look at such a happy product, the writer of the oak poem should withdraw his wooden sword and flee.

The comment is a clever display of wit, employing the language and imagery of the two poems. The subject of the haiku being colored leaves, the word "color" is repeatedly used in the sense of either "hue" or "colorful, unrestrained life" or both. Sanboku's image of a midwife prompted Bashō to use such phrases as "to give birth" or "a happy product," while that of an oak in Dasoku's poem induced him to say "wooden sword," comparing the poetry contest to a fencing match. The amusing cliché "come and look" in the second poem is slipped into the judgment, too, though in a totally different context. Also, though this does not show in English translation, Bashō used a number of puns. Unmistakably he was playing with a town wit's language, and very cleverly, too.

Yet, behind his playful pose, we can discern the nature of Bashō's critical consciousness. First of all, he liked the "unique conceit" of the midwife poem; he was amused by the original, if grotesque, association of a crimson maple leaf with the blood-stained hand of a midwife. Next, he preferred the world of colors to the colorless world; the first poem suggests the colorful life of a young libertine who knows both the brighter and darker sides of love, while the second poem recedes to the world of an old man who prefers an austere beauty. Thirdly, Bashō was drawn to the "vigorous language" of the first poem; Sanboku's words are the more lively and imaginative. All these preferences point in one direction. Bashō, at this stage, liked to see in a poem the manifestations of a youthful, vigorous imagination which knows no bounds in exploring the possibilities of human reality as the substance of poetry and of language as a means of expression. Bashō's critical commentaries throughout *The Seashell Game* are based on an attitude that favors the free expansion of man's life and fancy.

Bashō's tone of voice noticeably changes in *Haiku Contests in Eighteen Rounds*, to which he wrote the commentaries in the winter of 1678. The witty, playful, almost conceited tone of a town sophisticate is replaced by the more serious, thoughtful attitude of an established haikai master. This may be due in part to the likelihood that the participants in these contests, though most of them are not known today, were of a fairly high social status. It may also be due to the quality of the thirty-six contesting haiku, which by no means had the jolly tone of those in *The Seashell Game*. Yet there is no doubt that Bashō himself had grown as man and critic. Nearly seven years had passed since he compiled *The Seashell Game*, and during that period he had experienced a life of struggle in an unfamiliar city. Presiding over this new critical work is Bashō's awareness of the seriousness of his undertaking.

Haiku Contests in Eighteen Rounds consists of two contests, one in six rounds and the other in twelve. Here we shall examine the third round of the second contest. The two haiku, whose authorship is unknown, are about cherry blossoms:

Hanazakari *Yomo no shibai ya* *Aki no kure*	Blossoms at their best, But the theaters everywhere Are in an autumn evening.
Ueno irai *Aoba zo kaoru* *Boshun no yado*	Finally back from Ueno I smell green foliage at home Toward the end of spring.

The first haiku is about the loneliness of kabuki theaters in mid-spring, when everyone goes out to see cherry blossoms. The second is concerned with the scent of fresh green leaves after the colorful blossoms have fallen. Ueno (not to be confused with Bashō's home town), along with Yanaka, was an area of Edo noted for its cherry blossoms, and the poet, who roamed there every day during the blossom season, is now back at home and notices the fragrance of young leaves for the first time. Bashō, commenting on those two poems, wrote:

> Theaters become lonely when people crowd Ueno and Yanaka to admire fully blossoming cherry trees. Actors and theater-owners look as if they were part of a desolate nature scene, a scene that has neither cherry blossoms nor tinted leaves in it.[2] The comparison of deserted theaters to an evening scene in autumn is appropriate indeed, and I have a good deal of praise for this poem. Yet, as it happens, my student Sanpū has composed a haiku "The blossoms are heartless/ When they are in full bloom," which he has written on many a poetry card. Regrettable as it is, it must be said that the first haiku here is too similar to Sanpū's. As for the second poem, it presents the poet remembering the beauty of blossoms as he catches a remnant of their fragrance in a spring gale scattering the fallen petals.[3] The haiku has an elegant beauty that cannot be easily passed over, and I have therefore made it the winning verse. I still believe, however, that as a poem it is somewhat inferior to the first haiku.

Bashō gave a serious and sympathetic consideration to both these poems and passed judgment on them only after fully exploring their meaning. In the commentary he pays due respect to the traditional rules of poetry contests, but is not rigidly bound by them. He has made the second haiku the winner because the first poem violates a traditional rule: no poem can be a winner if it resembles an extant poem in subject matter or in motif. Yet Bashō frankly admits he likes the first poem better, for the reason that the comparison used in the poem is good. In this respect Bashō had not changed since the time of *The Seashell Game*, when he made the midwife poem the winner because of its highly imaginative comparison. But the nature of the two things compared here has nothing of that grotesqueness. The mood pervading both an empty kabuki theater and an autumn evening on the seashore is a somber and austere one. Evidently Bashō had begun to develop a taste for this type of beauty and had come to like it better than the elegant beauty that he admits exists in the green-foliage poem.

Two years later, Bashō judged another pair of poetry contests. One of his leading disciples at the time, Enomoto Kikaku (1661–1707), had composed fifty haiku, matched them in twenty-five rounds, and asked Bashō to comment. At about the same time, his disciple Sanpū did exactly the same. Kikaku's collection is called "The Rustic Haiku Contest" because the rival poems in each round are attributed to two imaginary rustics living on the outskirts of Edo. Sanpū's is entitled "The Evergreen Haiku Contest" since all the haiku in it involve plants that become green in various seasons of the year. These two contests were published in one volume under the general title *Haiku Contests (Haikai Awase)* in the autumn of 1680.

Bashō's critical attitude as revealed in this volume had changed further. In brief, he had become more versatile. A large number of critical ideas and idioms are employed in his judgments, and such terms as "rich," "tall," "strong," "elegant," "deeply felt," "profound," "eye-opening," "infinitely suggestive," and many more are used freely to describe certain poetic qualities. He borrowed terms and ideas abundantly from Japanese poetics, Chinese esthetics, Buddhism, and Taoism. For one thing, the verses by Kikaku and Sanpū were quite diverse in theme and style, very much like Bashō's own haiku at this time. The truth seems to be that Bashō was groping for new possibilities in criticism just as he was searching for a new style in his haiku composition. As a critic he was going through a period of experimentation, too.

There are, however, already some signs that suggest the direction Bashō was to take in his more mature years. For instance, here is the seventeenth round of "The Rustic Haiku Contest":

Kinuta no machi *Tsuma hoyuru inu* *Aware nari*	Pounding cloth in a town— A dog howls for his mate Piteously.
Imo uete *Ame o kiku kaze no* *Yadori kana*	A patch of taros outside. I listen to the sound of rain In the swirling wind.

Both poems appeal to the reader's auditory imagination. The first haiku focuses on a strangely sad harmony between the regular beat of fulling blocks and the irregular howl of a dog, both of which a lonely traveler heard one autumn evening. The second haiku concentrates on the sound of rain beating against large, soft taro leaves on a stormy night, as heard by a hermit sitting in his small hut. Commenting on these poems, Bashō had this to say:

> The first verse says "pounding cloth in a town" instead of the cliché "the village where they pound cloth." It also says "a dog howls for his mate" instead of using the more common line "a deer longs for its mate." It seems to me, however, that these are artifices within a work of art; too much craft has been expended here. On the other hand, I am greatly impressed by the mood of lonely devastation embodied in the sound of the rain beating against taro leaves. It approaches the sentiment expressed in Meng Shu-i's poem on rain, the last line of which is: "The rainwater dripping from the leaves makes a harmony with the moon as it falls on the banana leaves."[4] The second haiku should win the match.

The earlier Bashō, who took delight in imaginative comparisons, would have given victory to the first poem with its unique juxtaposition of a dog's howl and the sound of fulling blocks. But to the Bashō of 1680 it seemed too artificial. His liking was more for the lonely mood created by the sound of the rain falling on taro leaves. A taro leaf is like a banana leaf in that it is large, soft, and easily torn by wind and rain. The poem is in fact similar to Bashō's own haiku:

Bashō nowaki shite	A banana plant in the autumn gale—
Tarai ni ame o	I listen to the dripping of rain
Kiku yo kana	Into a basin at night.

This commentary clearly anticipates Bashō's steady move toward sabi. His poetic maturity was indeed not too far ahead. The year when he wrote commentaries to "The Rustic Haiku Contest" and "The Evergreen Haiku Contest" was the year that saw him settle down in the first Bashō Hut.

II *Later Critical Works*

Bashō's activities as a critical commentator must have greatly increased when he became a recognized haikai master. The number of his students grew large, and more and more people brought their verses to him for comment and advice. Yet as far as we know his later works of criticism are surprisingly few. After "The Rustic Haiku Contest" and "The Evergreen Haiku Contest," we can find him judging a poetry contest on only one occasion: in the autumn of 1687, he wrote critical commentaries for one of the four contests included in *The Extending Plain* (*Tsuzuki no Hara*). Besides that there are only two other works of criticism generally believed to be Bashō's: one, published in 1686, is commonly known as *Critical Notes on the New Year's Renku* (*Hatsukaishi Hyōchū*); the other, a very short work completed in 1693, is usually called *Autumn Night Critical Commentaries* (*Aki no Yo Hyōgo*). It may be that several others have been lost, but the general belief is that he virtually stopped writing criticism just when he came to formulate his own ideas about poetry. Evidently Bashō's disciples had this impression, and having had the privilege of hearing him talk, some of them attempted to record those of his conversations that touched on his art. We have a voluminous amount of these records today, most of them written after Bashō's death. Of these, the records by Kyorai and by Hattori Dohō (1657–1730) are most valuable, since they try scrupulously to be faithful to their master's words. The work of the other disciples by and large is less reliable, whether because of their faulty comprehension or because of their dogmatic tendency; but their notes are still valuable in that they represent Bashō as he was understood by his students. All in all, we do not suffer deeply from lack of material in glimpsing Bashō the critic in his later years.

As may be imagined, Bashō continued to cultivate a taste for a lonely, almost austere type of beauty, eventually making it one of his basic criteria for good poetry. There is plenty of evidence of this, but here we shall consider Bashō's own remark about one of the verses in *Critical Notes on the New Year's Renku.* The forty-seventh verse of this hundred-verse renku was contributed by one of seventeen participating poets, Kusakabe Kyohaku (16?-1696):

Inazuma no	A flash of lightning
Ko no ma o hana no	Through the trees, and the blossoms
Kokorobase	Are recalled to mind.

To this, Kifū added a couplet:

Tsurenaki hijiri	The nonchalant sage unpacks
No ni oi o toku	His satchel in the wilderness.

Bashō's comment on Kifū's verse is: "This verse is excellent in itself and in the way it is integrated with the preceding verse. On an ominously dark night with occasional flashes of lightning, a sage is going to sleep under the stars on the wild land. The essentials of a new haikai art lie in a verse like this." Kyohaku's lines picture a spectacular autumn night, with a flash of lightning so beautiful that for an instant the trees seem to have blossomed. This colorful beauty is unobtrusively toned down in Kifū's verse, which presents a Buddhist monk in a gray robe preparing to sleep in the wilderness. The monk, of course, recognizes the superhuman force in the flash of lightning as well as man's powerlessness before that force; nevertheless, he can nonchalantly settle down to sleep under the open sky. This monk must have come close to the image of an ideal man for the Bashō of 1686, who had come back from a long journey a few months earlier.

Bashō's esthetic preference is also observed in his critical commentaries in *The Extending Plain.* This anthology contains four haiku contests, each centering on one of the four seasons and judged by a different poet. Appropriately enough, Bashō judged the contest on winter themes, which consists of twelve rounds. Here is the fourth one, entitled "Withered Moor":

Matsunae mo	Young pine trees
Kareno ni medatsu	Conspicuous on a withered moor
Arashi kana	In the stormy wind.
	Kifū

Ōhashi o	A gigantic bridge
Kareno ni watasu	Over a withered moor:
Irihi kana	Beams of the setting sun. *Zenpō*

Bashō's comment is: "The first haiku reproduces the impression of an eye-catching scene where young pine trees gently waver in the wake of a wintry gust. The trees, small as they are, anticipate an arched beam as large as a rainbow. This is a highly expansive poem. The second haiku also presents a scene of withered moor that is difficult to pass over. But it seems less attractive than the pine tree poem." Kifū's haiku is very much like the couplet he wrote for the New Year's renku. Here again is an overpowering natural force threatening a frail existence which, however, shows little sign of resentment. Compared with Zenpō's colorful, large-scale poem, Kifū's haiku is somber and desolate. But Bashō felt no hesitation in giving it the laurels.

Another instance revealing Bashō's taste is seen in the eighth round of the same contest. Entitled "Icicles," this seems a better match than the fourth round:

Kaze ni kite	Brought by the wind
Tsurara ni sagaru	And hanging on an icicle,
Kaede kana	A maple leaf.
	Ittō

Kado tojite	Closing the entrance
Kankyo oshiyuru	And suggesting a leisurely life within,
Tsurara kana	The icicles. ***Kinpū***

Bashō's remark is: "A maple leaf hanging on an icicle is an exquisite scene that produces delicate, dry, sorrowful beauty. The second haiku, however, seems to be superior in sentiment as it shows the humble life of a leisurely man whose gate is kept closed by hanging icicles after the goose grass withered that blocked the doorway." Bashō, then, liked Ittō's poem insofar as it crystallizes winter beauty in the delicate image of a leaf frozen to a hanging icicle. But he did not like the colorfulness and loveliness of the tinted leaf, especially when compared with Kinpū's haiku, which focuses on the harsher aspect of winter. The second poem again portrays nature on a larger scale and in a more overpowering aspect.

Bashō's admiration for harsh, austere natural beauty is also reflected in a well-known episode first recounted by Kyorai in one of his letters. It occurred in late 1690 or early 1691, when Kyorai and Bonchō were compiling *The Monkey's Cloak* in Kyoto under Bashō's guidance. Kikaku, one of Bashō's leading disciples in Edo, had a haiku to contribute but could not make up his mind about its third line, so he wrote to his master to ask for help. As Bashō read it, the haiku was:

Shiba no to ya	On the brushwood gate
Jō no sasarete	A bolt is fastened—
Fuyu no tsuki	The winter moon.

Kikaku was wondering whether the last line had better read "The night frost." Bashō discussed the matter with Kyorai, and they came to the conclusion that the haiku, though acceptable, was not of an exceptionally high quality, and therefore that it made little difference which alternative was chosen. Eventually Bashō decided in favor of "The winter moon" and recommended the haiku for inclusion in *The Monkey's Cloak*. Then, some months later, he found he had misread the first line of Kikaku's poem because of the peculiar way the ideograms were written. The first line should have been read as "On this wooden gate." Bashō, who was away at the time, immediately wrote to Kyorai and said: "The reason why Kikaku had a hard time deciding on the third line is now quite clear. We must restore the first line. I do not know whether the engraving has already been completed, or whether fifty or one hundred copies have been printed; but I know we cannot sacrifice such an excellent poem because of that. If you have the printed copies there, destroy them and have new blocks made." Overruling Bonchō's objection, Kyorai followed his master's order. Today we can still see the traces of this last-minute correction in the original edition of *The Monkey's Cloak*.

So we have two versions of Kikaku's haiku. The restored version is:

Kono kido ya	On this wooden gate
Jō no sasarete	A bolt is fastened—
Fuyu no tsuki	The winter moon.

This is far more desolate in mood. The version with a brushwood gate suggests a peaceful country scene in winter, where a hermit is enjoying an idle life. But when the first line is changed to "On this wooden gate," that peaceful atmosphere is destroyed, for here is the sinister picture of a great castle pointing up to the dark winter sky. There is something heartless about the bolt tightly fastened on the wooden gate of the castle, and it perfectly complements the icy moon overhead. The mood is colder, harsher, and tenser.

However, alongside a liking for austere beauty Bashō also had a predilection for poems with simple, artless, "light" effects. We have already noted that he tried to write a haiku of "lightness" toward the end of his life, and we can easily imagine that this idea functioned as an important principle in his critical judgment. That principle was at work, for instance, when he criticized Etsujin's haiku on the New Year. According to Kyorai, who recorded the episode, the haiku in question was:

Kimi ga haru	Spring in His Majesty's reign—
Kaya wa moyogi ni	A mosquito net is light green
Kiwamarinu	Throughout the ages.

This is a panegyric praising His Majesty's reign which would keep the land in peace and happiness for ever and ever. Bashō did not like the poem and charged that it was "heavy in meaning." He would make it "lighter," he said, by changing the first line to "The moon's rays—" or "The dawning day—":

Tsukikage ya	The moon's rays—
Kaya wa moyogi ni	A mosquito net is light green
Kiwamarinu	Throughout the ages.

Thus corrected, the haiku becomes a poem about a mosquito net; the heavy, dignified tone almost like that of a national anthem has evaporated. What remains is the little discovery of an average townsman who, lying inside a mosquito net one evening, notices a unique harmony between the mellow whiteness of the moonlight and the light green of the net, both of which have remained unchanged throughout the centuries.

On another occasion Bashō applied the principle of "lightness" to a poem by Kyorai. As Kyorai himself tells the incident, he was trying to write a haiku on the Dolls' Festival. He had the material before his eyes: there were lovely little dolls, dressed in the costumes of ancient court nobles, sitting on a carpeted, tiered stand as if at a banquet. What especially attracted Kyorai's attention was that whoever had set up the stand had seated the dolls of the previous year on the lower tiers, while the more conspicuous upper tiers were occupied by the newer dolls. Thereupon he wrote the haiku:

Asamashi ya	What a shame!
Shimoza ni naoru	In the lower seats,
Kozo no hina	Last year's dolls.

But he did not feel the first line was very appropriate, and he tried to replace it with some other phrase, such as "How mortifying!", "Discolored hoods–," "Peach blossoms and willows–," and so forth. Satisfied with none of these, he finally amended the poem to read:

Furumai ya	A banquet–
Shimoza ni naoru	In the lower seats,
Kozo no hina	Last year's dolls.

Still, he found himself not completely satisfied. At his wits' end, he took the matter to his teacher and asked for help. Bashō answered: " 'A banquet–' is not quite satisfactory, indeed. But if you pick out a phrase with a deep sentiment for your first line, the poem will fall to the level of Shintoku's haiku, which often begin with 'The world of men–.'[5] You had better be content with what you have now." Bashō is again objecting to the use of emotion-loaded words. "Peach blossoms and willows–" would be too sentimental and too didactic also. "A banquet–," being more neutral, does away with sentimentalism and didacticism, and in that sense makes the poem "lighter" and better.

We have so far cited only negative examples, but of course there are some verses which Bashō approved of because of their "light" quality. One of these is a hokku by Itō Fugyoku (16?-1697), to which Bashō put a comment in the so-called *Autumn*

Night Critical Commentaries. The hokku is:

Bōzugo ya	A tonsured boy–
Atama utaruru	Bouncing off his head
Hatsu-arare	The year's first hail.

A little boy is happily hopping around in the first hailstorm of the year, not minding the stinging blows on his shaven head. Bashō's remark, addressed to Fugyoku, was: "Poems of recent times look heavy because they make too much use of sentiment. To avoid this, I depend on scenery in most of my verses. In this respect I was very much impressed to read this kind of verse by you." These words remind us of a poem of his own which he said had "lightness":

Ki no moto ni	Under the trees
Shiru mo namasu mo	Soup, fish salad, and everywhere
Sakura kana	Cherry blossoms.

In neither of these verses does the poet talk about *his* joy or sorrow, *his* love or hatred; it is an objective view, a scene of all-inclusive nature enveloping man and other things within itself.

According to Bashō's principle of "lightness" then, a poem should present a picture of life objectively in familiar words, avoiding intensely emotional expression. A poet should not pour his passions into his work; he should rather detach himself from the passion and submerge it within an objective scene. This is easy to say and difficult to practice–an inexpert poet often ends up composing a descriptive poem so plain and trite as to evoke no feeling at all. In this connection there is an interesting episode told by Kyorai. When he was yet a beginner, he asked his teacher how to compose a haiku. Bashō answered, "Write a concrete poem, and make sure that it has a haiku spirit." Whereupon Kyorai wrote:

Yūsuzumi	The evening cool–
Senki okoshite	I had an attack of lumbago
Kaerikeri	And returned home.

On reading the haiku Bashō burst into laughter, saying "This is not what I meant, either." Kyorai makes no comment on this episode, but its implications are sufficiently clear. The poem is "concrete" in that it depicts an incident; it has a bit of "haiku spirit," too, in that the little incident in a townsman's life is told in a calm, detached tone, a tone of "lightness." Yet the poem does not arouse any significant poetic feeling. The objective presentation of a familiar scene is not enough; it must be poetically suggestive. Here arises another of Bashō's critical principles, *yojō*, which might be literally translated as "surplus meaning."

"Surplus meaning" is a term age-old in Japanese literary criticism, dating back long before Bashō's time. Ordinarily, it was used to describe a poem that means more than its words say; there is a "suggested" meaning as well as a "stated" meaning. Traditional Japanese critics had often held that the merit of a poem is in proportion to its "surplus meaning." Bashō took over this concept and made repeated use of it in *Critical Notes on the New Year's Renku.* For example here are two successive verses from that renku, the first contributed by Kikaku and the second by Rika:

Fune ni cha no yu no *Ura aware nari*	A tea ceremony on the boat Along a beautiful coast.
Tsukushi made *Hito no musume o* *Meshitsurete*	As far as Tsukushi The kidnapped maiden Is to be taken.

Bashō wrote of Rika's verse:

This verse is perfect in terms of its theme and technique, as well as in the way it is linked to the preceding lines. A man with a good taste in art has kidnapped a maiden and is now making her perform a tea ceremony on his boat; the verse is a fresh departure from ordinary love verses and has much to be admired. Old stories, such as the one about Matsuura who kidnapped a princess, or the one about Lady Asukai who was forcibly taken away by a nobleman, are latent in the image of the man in the verse who is returning to Tsukushi.[6] The surplus meaning is infinite here.

Bashō is saying that he likes Rika's verse because the ancient tales in its background expand its meaning infinitely. The reader is led into the the world of *Taiheiki, The Tale of Sagoromo,* and other classics, and imagines various possibilities awaiting this poor girl, who is now following the ritual of tea on the boat.

Naturally Bashō gives a low mark to a poem that has little surplus meaning. One such example is a haiku by Kakei:

Tsuta no ha ya	Ivy leaves–
Nokorazu ugoku	Every one of them fluttering
Aki no kaze	In the autumn wind.

According to Kyorai, Bashō's criticism of this poem was: "A haiku should not say everything, as this one does." Another such example is a haiku by Hafū which Bashō came upon in an anthology:

Shitabushi ni	Could I but lie on my back
Tsukami-wakebaya	And clasp, branch by branch, the blossoms
Itozakura	Of the weeping cherry!

Bashō wondered why the compiler of the anthology had included such a verse. Kyorai volunteered to explain: "Doesn't it say everything that should be said about a weeping cherry tree in full bloom?" Bashō retorted: "Is there any good in saying everything?" Obviously he wanted the poet to suggest, and not to describe. If a verse says everything, it leaves no room for the reader's fancy; it does not induce him to undergo the experience himself. In Bashō's view, the very merit of the haiku form was that its extreme brevity enhanced poetic suggestiveness.

Within the haiku form, there are different ways to effect poetic suggestiveness. One is the use of allusion, as we have seen. Another is ambiguity: deliberate ambiguity increases a poem's evocative power. In this connection there is a revealing episode recorded by Dohō. Dohō once composed this haiku:

Hanadori no	A bird in the blossoms,
Kumo ni isogu ya	Hurrying to the clouds,
Ikanobori	A paper kite.

He brought the poem to his teacher and said: "I am afraid the meaning of this haiku won't be too clear to the reader. But, as soon as I revise it for the sake of clearer meaning, the poem becomes uninteresting. What shall I do?" Bashō advised that he leave it intact and read it as a poem about a paper kite. He then added: "A verse that has something interesting in it is acceptable, even though its meaning is not too clear. There are precedents in this matter." The ambiguity of Dohō's haiku comes from the fact that the subject of the verb "hurry" can be either the bird or the kite. There is a "leap" of meaning after each of the first two lines, and the meaning changes according to the reader's interpretation of the "leap." Bashō preferred to interpret the poem as that of a paper kite flying high up into the clouds, like a bird flying into "clouds" of blossoms, but he wanted the poet to leave it so that each reader might arrive at his own interpretation.

About this poetic "leap" Bashō had a good deal to say, especially in regard to the relationship between two consecutive verses of a renku. It is of course impossible to define the "leap" in clear-cut logical terms, and Bashō uses highly impressionistic words, such as "fragrance," "reverberation," "shadow," "reflection," and so forth. To take a well-known example cited by Kyorai, here are two verses from a certain renku:

Kureen ni *Gin-kawarake o* *Uchikudaki*	On the veranda A silver-glazed cup Is smashed to pieces.
Mi hosoki tachi no *Soru koto o miyo*	Look, how his slender sword Trembles, ready to leap!

The first verse suggests the scene of a banquet where a fierce quarrel has begun between two guests, one of them angrily smashing his wine cup on the veranda. The second verse, responding to the tension, creates an equally dramatic scene in which two antagonists are on the verge of a duel. Bashō's term defining the relationship between those verses is "reverberation," implying that as soon as one verse is struck the other reverberates from it, so to speak. The first verse, being so tense in mood, has made the following verse vibrate in sympathy. Kyorai tells us that Bashō, in explaining the nature of the link between these two verses, made the gesture of flinging a cup with his right hand while his left hand mimicked the act of reaching for one's sword.

Similarly, the term "fragrance" is used to define the nature of the relationship between two verses. Different disciples of Bashō cite different examples; here is one quoted by Zushi Rogan (16?-1693):

Kozue ikitaru	Revived at the top,
Yudachi no matsu	Pine trees in a summer shower.

Zensō no	A Zen monk
Akahadaka naru	Stark naked
Suzumi shite	Enjoying the coolness.

Certainly there is a resemblance between pine trees in the summer shower and a naked Zen monk enjoying the cool evening air. To Bashō and his disciples the nature of the resemblance could only be defined by an impressionistic term such as "fragrance." It is as if an ineffable fragrance were rising from the couplet and quietly flowing into the triplet.

The term "reflection" is used when a verse is thought to "reflect" the mood of its predecessor like a mirror. Bashō employed this term in connection with the following two verses in *Autumn Night Critical Commentaries*:

Yūzuki no	In the evening moon's
Oboro no mayu no	Dim light, her eyebrows show
Utsukushiku	Their beautiful shape.

Koshibagaki yori	From across the brushwood fence
Kagamitogi yobu	A mirror-polisher is calling.

The first verse sketches the elegant image of a lovely noblewoman sitting in the evening dusk. The second verse, reflecting that mood, indicates the leisurely life of such a lady in her tastefully decorated house, where the visitor is not a butcher or grocer but a decorous mirror-polisher! The word "polisher" also fits well with "the dim light" of the preceding verse.

As to the "leap" within a single haiku, Bashō and his disciples had less to say, though we can assume that such ideas as "fragrance," "reverberation," and "reflection" could be applied here as well. In this connection an interesting comment has been made by Dohō:

The writing of a hokku consists of grasping the movement of the mind that goes and then returns. This can be illustrated by a verse such as this:

Yamazato wa	In the mountain village
Manzai ososhi	Manzai dancers are late–
Ume no hana	Plum blossoms.

The poet first declares that in a mountain village Manzai dancers are late, and then he goes on to observe that plum blossoms are in bloom. His mind goes, and then returns. This is what happens in writing a hokku. If he were merely to say that in a mountain village Manzai men are late, that would make only an ordinary verse, a verse more properly placed in the main body of a renku. According to a certain book, the late Master said: "One should know that a hokku is made by combining things."

Here Dohō, probably following Bashō's teaching, seems to be saying that in an ordinary renku verse the meaning flows in only one direction, whereas in a hokku the direction of the flow is plural. A renku verse can be flat, because it can create tension by being linked to the preceding and following verses in various imaginative ways. But a hokku, coming at the beginning, cannot do this. The tension must be created within its own structure. Dohō does not spell this out, but apparently he implies that the tension within a hokku is similar to that between two succesive renku verses. And, of course, we can assume that what is true of a hokku is also true of a haiku.

Interesting also is Bashō's remark that a hokku, and therefore a haiku, "is made by combining things." This must refer to the technique of surprising comparison, which we observed earlier. But Dohō tries to explain it further by saying that it involves a certain movement of the mind: the mind "goes and then returns." That is a rather cryptic explanation which, however, is somewhat clarified by the example he cites. The haiku was written by Bashō in the spring of 1691, when he was visiting the "mountain village," his native Ueno. The "Manzai dancers" were a troupe who visited one house after another with congratulatory messages in the New Year's season. The first two lines of the haiku, then, present a peaceful spring scene in a mountain village where the tempo of life is slow and leisurely; indeed, the Manzai dancers who in a large city would come round before plum-blossom time are not here yet. This slow, leisurely movement of the mind wanders away toward the unseen dancers, encounters a lovely white image of plum blossoms, and in that instant turns and begins to flow back, eventually reaching the image of the mountain village again. In other words, the quiet, desolate atmosphere of the village suggested in the first two lines is redefined through the plum-blossom image in the third line. The beauty of plum blossoms is frigid, rustic, and lacking in gaiety; it is a fine complement to the spring scene of a countryside still devoid of the colorfully dressed dancers from the city. It is as if the image of plum blossoms were an echo of that of the mountain village.

In order that two things vibrate in unison, they must have roughly the same wave length. To further illustrate the relationship between two objects compared in a haiku, Dohō brings in another interesting poem by Bashō. It is about a special type of lay monks who go around town in midwinter singing hymns for forty-nine consecutive nights to commemorate the anniversary of St. Kūya's death:

Karasake mo	A dried salmon
Kūya no yase mo	And a Kūya pilgrim's gauntness,
Kan no uchi	Both in the coldest season.

Bashō was probably sitting in a house late at night, when he faintly heard a hymn sung by a passing Kūya pilgrim. He did not see the pilgrim, but he could visualize the haggard, gaunt figure of the ascetic and wanted to distill it into a haiku. He had a hard time doing so; "I toiled desperately for several days to capture the nature of that impression," he told Dohō later. He finally lit upon the image of a dried salted salmon, which seemed to share something basic with the lean lay monk. The impression of a dried salmon and that of a Kūya pilgrim were cold in a peculiar way, a way that cannot be expressed except through the images themselves. Bashō therefore joined the two images in his haiku and let tension generate from the juxtaposition. The reader's mind, first caught by the image of a dried salmon, "goes" to that of a lean Kūya monk trudging through the cold night, and then "returns" to the image of the salmon again. In the process the innermost nature of a Kūya pilgrim is expressed, and this without relying on abstraction.

Some of Bashō's disciples used the term "soul" to denote the innermost nature of an object. Ultimately, the purpose of the technique of surprising comparison employed in both haiku and renku is to crystallize the poet's glimpse of the "soul" of an object. The juxtaposition of a nude Zen monk and pine trees in a summer shower produces a "cool" impression that is of their essence; a Zen monk could not be compared to a dried salmon, because the latter's basic nature is "cold" rather than "cool." Kagami Shikō (1665–1731) illustrates this with another of Bashō's haiku:

Kinbyō no	On the golden screen
Matsu no furusa yo	How old the pine tree is!
Fuyugomori	Winter seclusion.

Replace the golden screen with a silvery one, and the haiku will fall to pieces. As Shikō rightly observes, a golden screen is "warm" in its inmost nature, while a silvery one is "cool." The haiku is an attempt to capture the warm "soul" of a man wintering at home, with a large standing screen keeping out the drafts. The screen is an old one and radiates the warmth of long familiarity. It has to be gold-colored.

It is of paramount importance to a poet, then, to catch the "soul" of his subject. He should not try to project his own emotion into the poem. He is a catalyst, a mere agent who leads an object to reveal its inner nature. In a famous passage on the poet's creative process, Dohō makes this point clear:

The Master said: "Learn about a pine tree from a pine tree, and about a bamboo plant from a bamboo plant." What he meant was that a poet should detach the mind from his own personal self. Nevertheless some poets interpret the word "learn" in their own ways and never really "learn." For "learn" means to enter into the object, perceive its delicate life and feel its feelings, whereupon a poem forms itself. A lucid description of the object is not enough; unless the poem contains feelings which have spontaneously emerged from the object, it will show the object and the poet's self as two separate entities, making it impossible to attain a true poetic sentiment. The poem will be artificial, for it is composed by the poet's personal self.

Elsewhere Bashō has distinguished between two types of poetic composition, "becoming" and "making." A good poet does not "make" a poem; he keeps contemplating his subject until it "becomes" a poem. A poem forms itself spontaneously. If the poet labors to compose a poem out of his own self, it will impair the "soul" of his subject. He should enter into the external object (the subject of his poem), instead of forcing it to come to him.

Beyond doubt, Bashō's idea of poetic composition is supported by his general philosophy of life, which we glimpsed in an early paragraph of *The Records of a Travel-Worn Satchel.* As we recall, his foremost tenet was "Return to nature." In his view, a civilized man is aware of the beauty of nature, while a barbarian is not. And nature is beautiful, because it knows of no conflict due to egoism. "Everything in nature," Bashō once wrote, "has its own fulfilment." A pine tree is content to lead its own life, and a bamboo plant faithfully follows its destiny; a pine never tries to become a bamboo, and a bamboo is never jealous of a pine tree's life. A poet observes each object of nature quietly following its predetermined course of life, and makes that observation a basic lesson in living his life as a man. If this is accepted, poetry, or a poetic mode of perception, becomes a moral discipline, almost a religion. Bashō, who once thought of becoming a monk, did not do so but clung to the thin line of poetry, no doubt because he thought poetry could solve problems that are usually the preserve of religion.

Could poetry ultimately become a religion for Bashō? Sadly, the answer seems to be in the negative. In a haibun written probably in 1692 he acknowledged the state of mind he eventually reached:

After wandering from place to place I returned to Edo and spent the winter at a district called Tachibana, where I am still though it is already the second month of the new year. During this time I tried to give up poetry and remain silent, but every time I did so a poetic sentiment would solicit my heart and something would flicker in my mind. Such is the magic spell of poetry. Because of this spell I abandoned everything and left home; almost penniless, I have barely kept myself alive by going around begging. How invincible is the power of poetry, to reduce me to a tattered beggar!

The "wandering" mentioned in the first line refers to his various journeys and visits between 1689 and 1691, which resulted in *The Narrow Road to the Deep North* and other masterpieces of poetry and prose. Poetically his wandering was a great success, but it did not give peace of mind as he had hoped it would. He felt he was a "tattered beggar," not only materially but also spiritually. The reason was that Bashō, who wanted to be liberated from all things on earth, could not free himself from the "magic spell" of poetry. He thought he could attain supreme serenity of mind by means of poetry, but, ironically, it was poetry itself that forever disturbed his mind. Toward the end of his life he is said to have called poetry "a sinful attachment." His deathbed poem of dreams roaming on a withered moor also seems to suggest Bashō's ultimate failure to enter a realm of religious enlightenment. Religion requires total passivity, whereas poetry, even such an impersonal form of poetry as the haiku, involves a measure of active participation on the part of the poet. Bashō, who considered poetry nothing more than a pastime in his youth, came to demand too much of it in his last years.

CHAPTER 6

The Permanence of Bashō

BASHŌ is said to have had more than two thousand students at the time of his death. If this number is debatable, there is no question about his position: few Japanese poets have enjoyed so high and so lasting a reputation. In the sense that he elevated the haiku into a mature literary form, Bashō was the very founder of a genre that was to prosper throughout the centuries. Indeed, the whole history of haiku could be said to be the history of his influence, for no poet after him could write a haiku without being aware of his presence. For that matter, Bashō's influence is very much alive today, for the haiku continues to thrive as never before. It is even becoming international—recent years have seen experimental writing in the haiku form in Western languages.

Such a pervasive influence must be attributed, above all, to the greatness of Bashō's literary works themselves, to the depth and scope of their probing into the reality of human life, as is universally the case with genuinely influential literary figures. Yet it is also due in no small measure to the many-sided nature of Bashō's literary genius; his poetry, developing through a variety of phases, appeals to people of widely varying tastes. His followers could find in him almost anything they sought—a town dandy, a youthful dreamer, a Buddhist recluse, a lonely wanderer, a nihilistic misanthrope, a happy humorist, an enlightened sage. The result has been a good deal of diversity in the nature of Bashō's influence in different periods and on different people. In the following pages we shall see how Bashō has been received by some of Japan's more important literary figures, as an indication of his impact on later literature.

I *Bashō's Influence Prior to the Twentieth Century*

Of all his numerous disciples, the poet who tried to follow Bashō with the most faith and devotion was probably Kyorai. A man of high integrity, he took the master's teaching to his heart with great enthusiasm. He became Bashō's student just when the sabi style was beginning to emerge and remained close throughout his teacher's peak period; in this sense he was the most characteristic product of the Bashō school of poetry. Bashō considered him highly trustworthy, too. Along with Bonchō, Kyorai was entrusted with the task of compiling the most prominent anthology of the Bashō school, *The Monkey's Cloak.* He was also the owner of the so-called House of Fallen Persimmons, where Bashō wrote *The Saga Diary.* The most characteristic features of Bashō's verse, their lonely mood and impersonal style, were adopted by Kyorai. In fact, virtually the only haiku on record to which Bashō is said to have applied the term sabi is a poem by Kyorai, which presents a distant view of two aged men engaged in idle talk under cherry blossoms:

Hanamori ya	The blossom guardsmen–
Shiroki kashira o	Their white-haired heads
Tsukiawase	Close together in a chat.

Many of his finer poems are like those of Bashō's prime in style and atmosphere. Here are two more of his haiku:

Ugoku to mo	Without appearing
Miede hata utsu	To move, a man tills the farm
Fumoto kana	At the foot of a hill.

Funanori no	Boatsmen are gone
Hitohama rusu zo	And the whole beach is vacant–
Keshi no hana	Poppy flower.

Yet, after all, Kyorai was not Bashō. He lacked, above all, his master's imaginative power and magic command of the language. As a consequence, his poetry is often smaller in scale and less moving in its emotional appeal. His personality was by no means dynamic, and this made him a faithful follower who would never leave his master behind.

Modest and self-critical, Kyorai never tried to become an influential haikai master. He accepted practically no students, so that when he died in 1704 there was no one left to propagate the style of Bashō's maturity. Steadily growing in popularity was a style more like that of his earlier period, a style more pedantic, witty, and consciously urbane. The poet who contributed a great deal to this new trend was Kikaku, one of the earliest disciples of Bashō and the compiler of *Shriveled Chestnuts*. Kikaku was close to Bashō to the end of his master's life, indeed, and he did write some fine poems in the sabi style—the haiku about taro leaves in the rain and about the wooden gate under the winter moon are two good examples. Yet his real preference was always for more colorful, sophisticated poetry like many of the verses collected in *Shriveled Chestnuts*. That liking came to be freely expressed after his master's death. The pedantic tendency was carried so far that some of his later poems were almost unintelligible. We can appreciate, for instance, this haiku which clearly shows the influence of the early Bashō:

Koe karete	Its shriek hoarsening,
Saru no ha shiroshi	The monkey's teeth are white—
Mine no tsuki	Over a peak, the moon.

But few readers have been able to make out the meaning of the next haiku, which Kikaku wrote in 1697 and which became one of his favorite poems:

Manjū de	With a bean-jam bun,
Hito o tazuneyo	Will you look for the man?
Yamazakura	Mountain cherry blossoms.

Unfortunately, this sort of verse became increasingly popular in the first half of the eighteenth century, partly because of Kikaku's high reputation among the verse-writing masses. Especially in Edo and other large cities where people took pride in their urbanity, the sort of haiku that play on riddles and juggling of words, as well as on bookish wit and whimsical conceits, were so overwhelmingly prevalent that Bashō's later poetic development was all but forgotten.

In contrast to Kikaku, those who became Bashō's students in his last years advocated "lightness" as their teacher's central poetic principle. Among them Shikō was the most influential, because more than any other student he was a literary theorist who wrote many treatises on the art of poetry. He also traveled far and wide, propagating his ideas of poetry among rural poets. But he became increasingly dogmatic in his poetic theory after his master's death, and his verses grew trite and uninspiring. We can see Bashō's influence on him in a haiku like this one:

Jikidō ni	On a temple's dining hall
Suzume naku nari	Sparrows twitter–
Yūshigure	Winter shower in the evening.

And we sense a bit of "lightness" in:

Kogatana no	I can't find
Sore kara mienu	That little knife
Tsugiki kana	Since the last grafting.

But this kind of poem is apt to be trivial and commonplace when written by a poet of no great talent, and far too often that was exactly what happened to Shikō and his followers. These rural poets who took as their model the poetry of Bashō's last period failed to carry on his ideal of "lightness," just as the urban poets who admired his early poetry failed to inherit his serious attempt to capture the "soul" of his poetic subject. The fifty years following Bashō's death thus became "the dark age of haikai."

What is known as the Haikai Restoration movement that took place in the second half of the eighteenth century was a revolt of the new age against such a degradation of poetry. Young poets who in many cases differed in taste and in some cases remained lifelong strangers, equally turned to Bashō's poetry in seeking poetic inspiration. Their common tenet was "Return to Bashō," which meant a stern rejection of the prevailing pedantry and triteness. Here are several of their haiku, all of which seem to show Bashō's influence:

Shii no mi no	The sound of an acorn
Itaya o hashiru	Rolling down the shingled roof–
Yosamu kana	Cold of the night.
	Hori Bakusui (*1718–83*)

Harusame no
Akahageyama ni
Furikurenu

Spring drizzle
Falling on a reddish clay hill;
The day comes to a close.
Matsuoka Seira (*1740–91*)

Kusa karete
Ushi mo aumuku
Shigure kana

The grass is withered
And a cow looks upwards, too—
Winter shower.
Katō Kyōtai (*1732–92*)

Behind these haiku there is the poet's perceptive eye trying to catch the essential nature of his subject. They are objective poems, expressly stating no passion on the poet's part. Using familiar vocabulary, they do not fall into frivolity.

Of the poets who joined the Haikai Restoration movement, by far the most talented was Yosa Buson (1716–84). Above all he had a rich imagination that could soar to the heights, which made him one of the rare poets capable of encompassing the full scope of Bashō's poetry. Always an ardent admirer of Bashō, he believed that "Bashō contained various types of poets in himself," and he endeavored to cover that whole range. For instance, he could write a haiku in the style of *Shriveled Chestnuts*:

Yanagi chiri
Shimizu kare ishi
Tokoro dokoro

Willow leaves have fallen,
Clear stream has dried, and the stones
Are scattered here and there.

He could follow the style of *The Narrow Road to the Deep North*, as seen in:

Samidare ya
Taiga o mae ni
Ie niken

Summer rains—
Facing an immense river,
A couple of houses.

He was skillful in a style reminiscent of *A Sack of Charcoal*, too:

Makumajiki
Sumai o nemono-
Gatari kana

Lying in bed,
The wrestler talks about the match
He shouldn't have lost.

Yet he distinctly differed from Bashō in some ways. The most important difference was that in the person of Buson there was usually a certain distance between the man and the poet. Buson, as a man living his daily life, was often remote from the reality presented in his poem. This is clearly seen when, for instance, his poem on summer rains is placed alongside Bashō's on the same subject:

Samidare o	Gathering the rains
Atsumete hayashi	Of summer, how swiftly flows
Mogami-gawa	The Mogami River!

Obviously Bashō is standing at the edge of the swift-flowing river, while Buson looks down at the river from a far-off hill—probably an imaginary hill. Bashō's mature haiku are mostly based on deeply felt emotion, whereas Buson often concocts a sentiment for his poem's sake. Bashō sought liberation from mundane life and expressed it in a poem whenever he actually attained it. Buson composed a poem about it and then escaped into that poem. This difference shows in their works.

The Haikai Restoration movement by Buson and his contemporaries, with their tenet "Return to Bashō," accelerated the trend toward Bashō idolatry which was already well under way at a more popular level. Various episodes about Bashō's life, many of them fictional, were published in numerous books hailing him as a divinely inspired poet. The Shinto headquarters officially deified him at the hundredth anniversary of his death, and the imperial court gave him a similar honor thirteen years later. Ironically, haikai itself went steadily downward in quality soon after Buson's death. It became nothing more than a hobby, a pastime, an ornament to urbane life, for most of those who wrote it. Its democratization resulted in its vulgarization. Thus in the nineteenth century an ever greater number of haikai poets came to admire Bashō's name, but there were few who could rightly claim to have inherited any aspect of his literary genius.

One notable exception to this degenerating trend was the work of Kobayashi Issa (1763–1827), who with his intense personality and vital language created shockingly impassioned verse. He is generally considered a most conspicuous heretic to the orthodox

Bashō tradition, because many of his renowned haiku are characterized either by fierce hatred of human evil voiced in a language of unrestrained passion, or by untainted love of children and small animals expressed in a language of childlike artlessness. Yet he, too, was an admirer of Bashō and wrote some haiku imprinted with the old master's influence:

Kogarashi ya *Ko no ha ni kurumu* *Shiozakana*	The wintry gust— Wrapped in a leaf, Salty relish.
Suzushisa ya *Nori no kawakanu* *Koandon*	How cool! The paste is not yet dry On a paper lantern.

Furthermore, Issa was more like Bashō than Buson in that poetry and life were at one in him. For Issa, a haiku was not the product of an exquisite fancy conjured up in a studio, but the vital expression of an actual life-feeling. Poetry was a diary of his heart; as a matter of fact, the two haiku we have seen appear in his diaries. In this sense Issa could more truly be said to be Bashō's heir than most of the haikai poets in the nineteenth century.

II *Twentieth-Century Images of Bashō*

The first free inflow of Western civilization to Japan took place dramatically toward the end of the nineteenth century, providing the Japanese with a chance to reconsider and re-evaluate their traditional, social, intellectual, and literary values. Haikai, then at the lowest ebb in its history, underwent a thorough reappraisal. One consequence of this was the destruction of the Bashō idolatry, and the destruction was rather too complete. In the opinion of some contemporary poets fervently aspiring to the type of freedom and individualism available in Western society, Bashō was one of the feudal institutions that unduly bound their creative urge. Buson seemed a more attractive figure, because he was more unfettered in his imagination and more daring in his sensual expression, while Bashō appeared to be looking backward to Saigyō and other medieval ascetics. The devaluation of

Bashō and elevation of Buson, eloquently proposed by Masaoka Shiki (1867–1902), profoundly affected many haiku poets in succeeding decades. On the other hand, the fall of Bashō as a haikai god had the effect of freeing him from the narrow haiku world. His poetry began to attract the serious attention of writers outside of the haiku poets' circles, who could now more freely form their own images of Bashō. Bashō's influence widened in scope as soon as he was toppled from the sacred pedestal.

The first new image assigned to Bashō was that of a Japanese Romantic, an image envisaged in the last years of the century by a group of young poets who heralded a new age in the history of Japanese poetry. For a millennium Japanese poetry had largely been confined to the rigid forms of tanka and haikai; these revolutionaries broke down that convention and brought it closer to the freer forms of Western verse. These "new style" poets were ardent followers of Western Romantic poets, such as Wordsworth, Shelley, Keats, Byron, Heine, Goethe, and Hoffmann, and they saw in Bashō a Japanese version of their Western models. In their view he was a social misfit, an introverted dreamer and an eternal wanderer in search of a mystic union with the heart of some superhuman power lying beyond the reach of the human intellect. It was natural that they, writing in Japanese, sometimes echoed that haikai poet when creating Japanese counterparts to Western Romantic heroes. For instance, "The Poem of Hōrai" ("Hōrai Kyoku") by Kitamura Tōkoku (1868–94), a dramatic poem inspired by Byron's "Manfred," employs images reminiscent of Bashō in depicting its wandering hero:

> Since leaving the capital
> My aimless journey, how many springs and autumns?
> That ever unstoppable traveler, Time, meant little to me.
> Straw sandals, I liberally changed
> From an old pair to a new one, each pair stamping
> My footprints that remained forever behind me . . .

A similar image of a lonely traveler appears in two of the most celebrated modern Japanese poems, "By the Old Castle at Komoro" ("Komoro naru Kojō no Hotori") and "Song of Travel on the Chikuma River" ("Chikuma-gawa Ryojō no Uta") by

Shimazaki Tōson (1872–1943), who belonged to the same Romantic group as a young poet. Tōson, whose birthplace was near the setting of *A Visit to Sarashina Village,* was a lifelong admirer of Bashō and once took time out to write an essay on his haiku. As a youth he went on a wandering journey along roughly the same route that Bashō had taken two centuries earlier. There is even a theory that his pen name, literally meaning "wistaria village," was derived from one of Bashō's haiku.

After a short season of Romanticism, the "new style" of Japanese poetry went through an extensive period of Symbolism under the influence of Baudelaire, Verhaeren, Mallarmé, Verlaine, Rossetti, and others. Not surprisingly, Bashō then came to be considered a Symbolist. According to the modern Japanese Symbolist poets, Bashō ventured deep into the forest of nature and had mystic "correspondences" with it. He was aware, they said, of the interrelatedness of all things in the universe and tried to suggest it by Symbolist means such as synesthesia. In the preface to a poetry collection which marked the beginning of the Symbolist period in modern Japanese verse, Kanbara Yūmei (1876–1952) calls Bashō's haiku "the most Symbolic of all Japanese literature"; the very title of the poetry collection, *Birds of Spring* (*Shunchōshū*), is borrowed from Bashō. Another leading Symbolist poet, Miki Rofū (1889–1964), included an essay on Bashō in one of his books of verse with the remark that Bashō's haiku "have a Symbolist mood, if we express it in our words." The most colorful of all Japanese Symbolists, Kitahara Hakushū (1885–1942), wrote several poems on Bashō, one of which echoes his dictum "Learn about a pine tree from a pine tree, and about a bamboo plant from a bamboo plant":

> A poem is something spontaneous,
> Something of life.
> Because of a pine tree, the wind of pine.
> Because of a pasania tree, the cool breeze of pasania.

The same idea is reflected in a more distinctly Symbolist poem by Hakushū, entitled "Platinum Correspondences":

> Birds, beasts, various fish and shellfish:
> May they all accept themselves as they are!

Stars, mountains, clouds, rains and storms:
May they all perfume themselves as they are, too!

Then, may the senses of trees and grass
Correspond with the sorrowful feelings of mankind!

Here the "correspondences" of Bashō are merged with their counterparts in Western Symbolism. Hakushū, together with some other Japanese Symbolist poets of his time, leaned more and more toward Bashō as he grew older.

The Symbolist movement in Japanese poetry had its counterpart in the novel, in the so-called Neo-Sensualist movement that flourished in 1920s. A reaction against Naturalistic Realism that emphasized scientific accuracy in describing the cold facts of life, the new movement insisted that the foremost technique of the novel should be the symbolization of sensory perceptions which pierce through the facts. "In brief," explained its cheif exponent, Yokomitsu Riichi (1898–1947), "the New Sensualist's 'sensuous symbol' refers to that which is catalyzed by an intuition of the subject which has jumped into the object after peeling off its natural exterior." Most likely the idea was inspired by fashionable Western literary and esthetic movements such as Futurism, Cubism, Expressionism, Dadaism, as well as Symbolism, but it unquestionably resembles Bashō's notion that the poet "enters into the object, perceives its delicate life and feels its feelings, whereupon a poem forms itself." In fact, Yokomitsu said he found "sensuous symbols" in Bashō's poetry, which he regarded very highly. His characteristic prose style seems to share some basic quality with Bashō's haiku, too. The last two sentences of the following passage, taken from one of his short stories, provide an example:

At the edge of the veranda Kaji and Takada immediately began composing haiku on the assigned topic of the day, "Arrowroot Flowers." Kaji was sitting with an open notebook on his lap, his back turned toward the interior of the house and his body leaning against a pillar. He felt as if his weariness were being absorbed into the green of the oranges that casually touched one another on the drooping branches. A cicada's incessant cry reverberated through the air, reaching the evening sky that still reflected the brightness of the sea below.

Certainly here are a Symbolist's "correspondences," but they are closer to Bashō's than to Baudelaire's. As a matter of fact, all the main characters of this story, including Kaji and Takada, are haiku writers. Yokomitsu himself was fond of writing haiku and composed a considerable number. It was only natural that he should apply typical haiku techniques, such as surprising comparison and the merging of the senses, to the writing of fiction.

Modern Japanese novelists, however, were in general more interested in Bashō as a man who tried to find in poetry a substitute for religion. Living in an age when religion had lost its redemptive power, they saw in Bashō a forerunner of the modern man who squarely faced the question: "How shall we live in a society where there is no religion to provide a basic system of values?" For instance, Kōda Rohan (1867–1947), one of the major writers in the formative years of modern Japanese fiction, sometimes created a hero whose most basic principle of conduct is his artistic impulse and who, because of that devotion, attains a final victory over his rivals. Such estheticism must be attributed to various sources, but Bashō's way of life was very likely Rohan's chief inspiration. When Rohan was suffering a period of frustration as a writer in his early twenties, he often set out to wander with a book of Bashō's poems. His pseudonym, meaning "with the dew," originated in a haiku he composed on one of those journeys:

Sato tōku	Villages are far—
Iza tsuyu to nen	Let me sleep with the dew,
Kusamakura	Making the grass my pillow.

The following poem, which he wrote on another of those journeys, also echoes Bashō's haiku on chestnut blossoms, though as a poem the model is distinctly superior to the imitation:

Tōtosa yo	How noble!
Nani fuzei naki	With no affectation whatever,
Kuri no hana	Chestnut blossoms.

Indeed, many of the artists Rohan depicts with affection in his novels seem ordinary and unostentatious except when they face critical moments in their artistic careers. Rohan himself, however, seems to have been continually disturbed by a conflict between literary ambition and Buddhistic serenity of mind, as was the case with Bashō. Probably that is why this haiku has a rather self-debasing tone: the poet is *wishing* he could be like a chestnut blossom. It was no accident that in his later years Rohan virtually gave up writing fiction and devoted himself to an intensive study of Bashō.

A modern Japanese novelist who was even more painfully conscious of the unbridgeable chasm between life and the ideals of art, Akutagawa Ryūnosuke (1892–1927), also had a profound interest in Bashō as a man anticipating the dilemma of the modern artist. In a long essay on Bashō he refers to the poet's attachment to his art and writes:

> Goethe said that whenever he set out to write a poem he became possessed of a daemon. Wasn't Bashō also too much at the mercy of a poetic daemon to become a recluse? To rephrase the question, wasn't the poet more overpowering than the recluse in the person of Bashō? I am fascinated with the dilemma of that man who could not completely become a recluse. I am also fascinated with the fact that his dilemma was such a dire one.

Akutagawa wrote some fine stories dramatizing the dilemma. The most notable, "Hell Screen" (Jigoku Hen"), portrays a demoniac painter who seems capable of any evil if necessary for his art's sake. Eventually the painter is trapped; he is driven to sacrifice his beloved daughter in the interest of his art. The artist-heroes in Akutagawa's stories are closer to Bashō than those in Rohan's in that they do not enjoy a happy denouement made possible by the eventual union of life and art. For Akutagawa the dilemma was insoluble: if the artist chooses to place his art ahead of his life, in the end he must suffer the destruction of his life.

The image of Bashō as the forerunner of modern poetry began to be recognized by recent haiku poets, too. Especially the Humanist poets in 1940s made it their ultimate poetic aim to probe into the depths of human nature and to discover a meaningful way of living, and in doing so they saw their great model in Bashō. Their leader, Nakamura Kusatao (b. 1901), calls Bashō "Japan's first modern poet" and goes on to explain:

In that he marked the very first step toward "art for life's sake" and in that he empirically discovered the dignity of his living self and tried to grasp universal truths of life by penetrating through his personal ego into the innermost part of his being—in other words, in that he tried to pursue a "positive life" based on his conviction of what lay in his innermost self, we see how truly Bashō anticipated the "modern age."

It is in this way that Kusatao tries to follow Bashō in his own creative activities. In many of his finer haiku there is the image of a man desperately searching the road to salvation in the age of anxiety and restlessness. For example:

Michinoku no *Mimizu mijikashi* *Yamasaka-gachi*	In the deep north Earthworms are short— Sloping mountain road.
Hiyu morotomo *Shinkō kiete* *Kareno no hi*	Together with metaphors Disappears my faith— Sun over a withered moor.
Ennetsu ya *Shōri no gotoki* *Chi no akarusa*	Scorching heat— How like a victory, The earth's brightness.

Kusatao and his group made an immediate impact on the haiku writing of the day. Since then, Japanese haiku in general can be said to have been moving steadily from Buson's shade to Bashō's. The trend is very likely to continue because poetry of the future, in whatever form it may be written, will not be permitted to serve as an idle pastime isolated from other activities of life. Japanese literature since World War II has been characterized by its social and moral consciousness, and the haiku is no exception.

With the increasing interest in the haiku outside Japan, Bashō's influence can be said to be becoming international. Western poets and artists for whom haiku became a source of inspiration in one way or another had read, not the modern haiku which began with Shiki at the turn of this century, but the classical haiku which evolved around Bashō's poetic principles. Moreover, Bashō was the first to fully explore the poetic possibilities of the haiku form, and anyone inspired by that form is indirectly indebted to Bashō for having made haiku what it is. The structure of superposition, developed by Ezra Pound under the influence of haiku, is in essence Bashō's "leap" technique, a method based on "the movement of the mind that goes and then returns." The same method is also partly accountable for the technique of montage in the modern film heralded by Sergei M. Eisenstein, who once called haiku "montage phrases." John Gould Fletcher liked the objectivity of haiku and felt the need of this quality in contemporary English poetry; this objectivity, too, goes back to Bashō, who insisted on learning about a pine tree from a pine tree and about a bamboo plant from a bamboo plant. As more and more Western poets write haiku or haiku-like poems in their languages, Bashō's influence on them through the haiku form will become diluted, often to the extent that it will disappear from their poetry. That is what is expected; in fact, that is precisely what Bashō wished for. He always encouraged his students to cultivate their individual talents rather than to follow him with blind faith. Several months before his death he wrote a haiku and gave it to one of his students:

Ware ni nina	Do not resemble me—
Futatsu ni wareshi	Never be like a musk melon
Makuwauri	Cut in two identical halves.

Notes and References

Chapter One

1. One of the more recent theories has it that Bashō was first hired as a butler or a clerk in charge of provisions in Yoshitada's household.

2. Kawai Sora (1649–1710) was a student Bashō was very fond of. He lived close to the Bashō Hut and served as a companion in his teacher's daily life. No doubt it was because he had such a close relationship that Bashō often chose him to travel with him.

3. The Japanese used a lunar calendar until 1873, their year starting about a month later than the corresponding Gregorian calendar year. In a normal year, the eighth of the twelfth month would fall sometime late in October or early in November.

4. Sun Ching, a scholar of the Three Kingdoms period, spent all his days reading books in a locked room. It is said that he often had a rope tied around his neck lest he doze off during his all-night reading. Tu Wu-lang, an eccentric Sung scholar, also lived behind locked doors. One book says that for thirty years he never went outside his house.

Chapter Two

1. Compare the number with those of two other distinguished haiku poets: Buson wrote about three thousand haiku, and Issa, more than twenty thousand.

2. There is a haiku on the Year of the Bird which an early biography attributes to Bashō at the age of thirteen. Today's Japanese scholars, however, have serious doubts as to its authenticity.

Chapter Three

1. Like Saigyō, Nōin (989-?) was a Buddhist monk who wrote some excellent tanka. He traveled a great deal; many of his poems are based on his experiences during these journeys.

Chapter Four

1. A reference to an epigrammatic sentence in *Chuang-tzu*: "A little dove laughs at a phoenix." It is a derisive comment on a small-minded person incapable of understanding a great man.

2. The Bashō Hut was located near the point where the Hakozaki River branches off from the Sumida River.

3. A reference to one of the eight poems by Tu Fu (712–70) collectively entitled "Autumn Meditation," which includes the line: "Meeting the bloom of chrysanthemums for the second time, I shed nostalgic tears over the bygone days."

4. Sugiyama Sanpū (1647–1732), a wealthy fish merchant, was one of Bashō's earliest disciples in Edo and helped him through his early years in that city. Little is known about Kifū and Taisui, though both were Bashō's teammates in the composition of several important renku.

5. A biwa is a musical instrument, probably Indian in origin, which came to Japan through China around the eighth century. Somewhat like a guitar in appearance, it usually has four strings and is from two to three feet long.

6. One version, entitled "A Prose Poem on the Unreal Dwelling" ("Genjū-an no Fu"), is written in an equally accomplished style. Today's Japanese scholars generally agree that the "Essay" is a later and more definitive version than the "Poem," mainly because the former is the version published in *The Monkey's Cloak*.

7. In his poem "Meditating over the Past," Po Chü-i (772–846) wrote how exhausting his verse-writing endeavors had been. A poem attributed to another famous Tang poet, Li Po (701–62), says Tu Fu had become lean due to his long-sustained effort to produce good verses.

8. Tani Bokuin (1646–1725), head of a rich family that operated a shipping firm in Ōgaki, was an old friend of Bashō's. They may already have known each other in 1660s, when they both studied haikai in Kyoto.

9. Musashi Plain is an extensive plain located in Musashi and its neighboring provinces. Edo was its largest and most important city.

10. Tu Fu, in a poem called "A Visit at Fenghsien Temple in Lungmen," wrote: "Near awakening, I hear the bells of dawn/That lead any man into deep meditation."

11. Sei Shōnagon (966-1025?), in her famous *Pillow Book* (*Makura no Sōshi*), wrote of the anguish she experienced when she was unable to compose a poem on a cuckoo-hearing expedition.

12. Iio Sōgi (1412–1502) was one of the most influential writers of linked verse and, like Bashō, was a lifelong traveler. Sesshū (1420–1506), a Zen monk, was renowned for his black ink painting. Sen Rikyū (1522–91) was highly acclaimed as the tea master who brought his art to a new level of artistic attainment by creating an esthetic of austerity.

13. Ki Tsurayuki (868–946?), a leading poet and critic in his time, wrote *The Tosa Diary* (*Tosa Nikki*) describing his voyage from Tosa Province to Kyoto. Kamo Chōmei (1153–1216), a noted poet and essayist, was believed in Bashō's time to be the author of a thirteenth-century travel journal called *Journey to the Eastern Barrier* (*Tōkan Kikō*). The nun Abutsu (?-1283) recorded her journey from Kyoto to Kamakura in her *Diary of the Waning Moon* (*Izayoi Nikki*).

14. Sung poets Huang Shan-ku (1045–1105) and Su Tung-p'o (1036–1101) were known for their novel conceits and fresh poetic idiom.

15. Gyōki (668–749) was one of the most respected priests in the prime years of Buddhism in Japan. He traveled around the country building bridges and dams, creating better roads and erecting temples.

16. The poem was written by Ōtomo Yakamochi (716?–85) in 749, when gold was presented to the imperial court from the people in the far north. It sang of "flowers of gold" blooming on Mount Michinoku, a place popularly believed to be Kinkazan.

Chapter Five

1. *The Winter Sun, The Monkey's Cloak, A Sack of Charcoal,* and other haikai anthologies of the Bashō school were all published by his disciples, with their names appearing as compilers. *The Narrow Road to the Deep North* and other journals by Bashō were never published in his lifetime. Bashō published *The Seashell Game* some time after his arrival in Edo.

2. A reference to a celebrated tanka by Fujiwara Teika (1162–1241):

Miwataseba	As I look ahead
Hana mo momiji mo	I see neither cherry blossoms
Nakarikeri	Nor crimson leaves:
Ura no tomaya no	Only a modest hut on the coast
Aki no yūgure	In the dusk of autumn evening.

3. An allusion to a tanka by Priest Jakuren (?–1202):

Chiri ni keri	They have all fallen.
Aware urami no	Oh, of whom are you resentful,
Tare naraba	Mountain Gust of Spring?
Hana no ato tou	You seem so eager to visit
Haru no yamakaze	With the blossoms after they are gone.

4. The poem, entitled "Summer Rain," appears in an anthology of

Chinese verse widely circulated in Bashō's time. Little is known about Meng Shu-i.

5. Itō Shintoku (1633–98) often wrote poems generalizing the ways of the world. An example:

Hito no yo ya	The world of men—
Futokoro ni masu	Perched in a peddler's bosom,
Wakaebisu	Gods of Wealth for the new year.

6. A medieval war chronicle *Taiheiki* describes how a samurai from Tsukushi (northern Kyushu) named Matsuura Gorō became infatuated with a princess and kidnapped her at a port near Osaka. *The Tale of Sagoromo* (*Sagoromo Monogatari*), an eleventh-century court romance, contains an episode about the seduction of Lady Asukai by a nobleman who took her to Tsukushi against her will.

Index

(Haiku are listed by their first lines.)